The Nikkormat Book

FOCAL CAMERA BOOKS

THE ASAHI PENTAX BOOK	*Clyde Reynolds*
THE MINOLTA XE-1 & SR-T BOOK	*Clyde Reynolds*
THE NIKKORMAT BOOK	*Clyde Reynolds*
THE PRAKTICA BOOK	*Leonard Gaunt*

FOCAL CAMERA GUIDES

ASAHI PENTAX GUIDE 18th ed.	*W. D. Emanuel*
BOLEX H8 H16 GUIDE 9th ed.	*A. J. Surgenor*
CANONET GUIDE 5th ed.	*W. D. Emanuel*
CANON REFLEX GUIDE 4th ed.	*W. D. Emanuel*
EXAKTA 35 mm. GUIDE 10th ed.	*W. D. Emanuel*
HASSELBLAD GUIDE 4th ed.	*W. D. Emanuel*
KONICA COMPACT 35 mm GUIDE 1st ed.	*W. D. Emanuel*
KONICA REFLEX GUIDE 6th ed.	*W. D. Emanuel*
LEICA GUIDE 44th ed.	*W. D. Emanuel*
LEICAFLEX GUIDE 4th ed.	*A. Matheson*
MAMIYA SEKOR SLR GUIDE 3rd ed.	*W. D. Emanuel*
MINOLTA SR GUIDE 9th ed.	*W. D. Emanuel*
MINOX GUIDE 8th ed.	*W. D. Emanuel*
MIRANDA GUIDE 2nd ed.	*W. D. Emanuel*
NIKON GUIDE 4th ed.	*W. D. Emanuel*
NIKKORMAT GUIDE 5th ed.	*W. D. Emanuel*
OLYMPUS OM-I GUIDE 2nd ed.	*W. D. Emanuel*
OLYMPUS 35 mm. COMPACT GUIDE 1st ed.	*W. D. Emanuel*
PRAKTICA PRAKTICAMAT GUIDE 8th ed.	*W. D. Emanuel*
RETINA GUIDE 24th ed.	*W. D. Emanuel*
RETINA REFLEX GUIDE 6th ed.	*W. D. Emanuel*
RETINETTE GUIDE 8th ed.	*W. D. Emanuel*
ROLLEICORD GUIDE 6th ed.	*W. D. Emanuel*
ROLLEIFLEX GUIDE 39th ed.	*W. D. Emanuel*
ROLLEI 35 mm. GUIDE 2nd ed.	*W. D. Emanuel*
YASHICA GUIDE 7th ed.	*W. D. Emanuel*
YASHICA 35 mm. GUIDE 4th ed.	*W. D. Emanuel*

THE NIKKORMAT BOOK

for EL and FT2 users

CLYDE REYNOLDS

AMPHOTO

Garden City, New York 11530

ISBN–0–8174–0627–1
Library of Congress Catalog Card No: 75–15132

First Edition 1976

Text set in 10 pt. Photon Times, printed by photolithography,
and bound in Great Britain at The Pitman Press, Bath

Contents

Where to look for . . .

The single lens reflex

In a single lens reflex camera, the single lens both focuses light onto the film, and forms the viewfinder image. Except at the instant of taking the picture, light passing through the lens is reflected by a mirror set at 45° to form an image on a ground glass screen above the mirror box. While the film is being exposed, the mirror moves out of place, resulting in complete blacking out of the viewfinder image. For viewing, the mirror is exactly mid way between the film plane and the viewfinder screen, so the image is exactly what will be recorded on the film if a picture is taken. It shows the area of subject covered (allowing a small margin for framing tolerances) whatever lens is fitted to the camera, and the exact focus.

On early single lens reflex cameras, this image was always viewed at waist (or chest) level, but most modern models allow eye-level viewing. This is achieved usually through a five-sided pentaprism—or roof prism—which also turns the image back the right way round. Some cameras allow the pentaprism to be exchanged for other types of viewfinder, but on most 35 mm reflexes, like the Nikkormat, it is a permanent fixture.

The eyepiece is fitted with a magnifying lens so that the image on the screen appears about 25 inches from the eye, and nearly life size with the standard lens fitted to the camera.

The 35 mm single lens reflex

TOP
1 Subject
2 Lens
3 Diaphragm
4 Viewing Screen
5 Pentaprism
6 Eyepiece
7 Pressure Plate
8 Mirror
9 Film
10 Image seen in viewfinder

BOTTOM
The film records exactly what was seen in the viewfinder, with just a little bit more to allow for slide mounts or negative masks slightly smaller than the image area on the film.

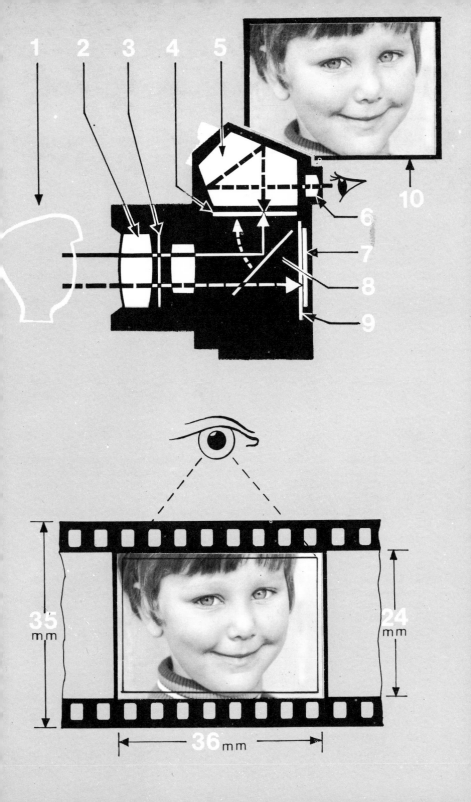

1 2 3 4 5

6
7
8
9

10

35 mm

24 mm

36 mm

Nikkormat cameras

The Nikkormat cameras are 35 mm single lens reflexes with fixed eye level pentaprisms, focal plane shutters, bayonet mounted interchangeable lenses and through-the-lens exposure measurement.

This guide covers the Nikkormat FT2 and Nikkormat EL.

The Nikkormat FT2 is a through-the-lens metering camera, which features full aperture metering (using lenses with coupling prongs). The meter is coupled to the shutter speed and lens aperture and a needle, visible in the viewfinder, is lined up with a cut-out. There is also a read-out on the top plate. It has shutter speeds from 1 to 1/1000 sec, displayed in the viewfinder. There is a built-in self-timer, a mirror lock, a depth-of-field preview button, a hot shoe and a 3 mm (PC) flash contact. M or X synchronisation is selected with the shutter speed. The focusing screen has a central split-image rangefinder spot surrounded by a microprism collar. The standard lens is usually chosen from the 55 mm f1.2, 50 mm f1.4, 50 mm f2 IC Nikkors or the 55 mm f3.5 Micro Nikkor. Recent lenses have a standardized 52 mm filter screw.

The Nikkormat EL is a through-the-lens metering camera with optional fully automatic shutter speed selection. The meter needle indicates the required shutter speed on a scale in the viewfinder. Manually set speeds are also shown on this scale. Shutter speeds from 4 seconds to 1/1000 are available set either automatically or manually.

There is a built-in self-timer, a mirror lock, and a depth-of-field preview button. The synchronization (M or X) of the 3 mm (PC) and accessory shoe flash contact is set with a ring round the shutter setting knob. The normal focusing screen has a built-in split image and microprism rangefinder. The standard lenses are normally chosen from the 55 mm f1.2, 50 mm f1.4, 50 mm f2 Nikkors or 55 mm f3.5 Micro-Nikkor.

Other Nikkormats

Nikkormat cameras were developed from Nikkorex cameras. The FTN was like the FT2, but had no hot shoe, and twin 3 mm (PC) flash contacts. The film speed selector had no lock mechanism. The Nikkormat FT differed from the FTN by taking its meter reading evenly from the whole focusing screen area, and requiring the film speed to be set manually to the maximum aperture of any lens in use. The Nikkormat FS is a similar camera without a built-in meter. Most of the information in this book applies to all Nikkormats. In some areas, Nikkormat cameras are sold under the name of Nikomat.

Other Nikon SLRs

The other major range of Nikon cameras are the F, F2 and F2S. These are larger and heavier than the Nikkormats. They have horizontally-running shutters, interchangeable viewfinders, and can be fitted with motor drives and other accessories. However, they use the same range of lenses and behind-the-lens accessories (bellows, tubes etc.). The Nikon F2 and F2S cameras are covered in another book in this series.

Nikkormats

TOP EL.
BOTTOM FT2.

EL

FT-2

Nikkormat EL

The Nikkormat EL is a 35 mm single lens reflex with eye-level viewfinder, fitted with a fully automatic focal plane shutter. The shutter speeds (between 4 and 1/1000 second) are set automatically (although alternatively may be selected manually).

Externally, this feature is characterised by the automatic (A) setting position on the shutter speed dial, and the battery testing light on the back of the top plate.

To provide the power for the exposure system, a silver oxide battery is housed below the instant return mirror.

A flash terminal is fitted to the camera body, and there is a 'hot shoe' contact on top of the pentaprism, allowing the use of cordless flash units. The synchronisation is set with the outer ring of the shutter speed knob.

EL Features

1	Frame counter	15	Aperture and focus index
2	Film transport lever	16	Focus ring
3	Shutter release button	17	Depth-of-field scale
4	Film speed dial	18	Aperture scale
5	Film speed index	19	Neck strap lug
6	Eyepiece	20	Self-timer/exposure hold
7	Flash contact	21	Lens
8	Film speed lock	22	Stop-down button
9	Film speed scale	23	Meter coupling
10	Rewind crank	24	Mirror lock
11	Back release catch	25	Lens release button
12	Accessory shoe	26	Rewind release button
13	Aperture setting ring	27	Tripod bush
14	Meter coupling prong		

Nikkormat EL

With the 50 mm $f2$ lens, the Nikkormat EL weighs 985 g. (2 lb 2 oz). When the 55 mm $f1.2$ lens is fitted, the weight is increased to 1200 g (2 lb 10 oz). The body alone weighs 780 g (1 lb 1 oz) and is 145 mm ($5\frac{2}{3}$ in) wide, 94 mm ($3\frac{11}{16}$ in) high, and 55 mm ($2\frac{1}{4}$ in) thick.

The camera uses 35 mm film, either in film manufacturers' cassettes, or in reloadable cassettes. It does not use the cassettes designed for the Nikon F or F2 cameras. The picture is the standard 24 × 36 mm size. A pressure plate and roller accurately registers the film against the gate.

The metered exposure times, and the manually set shutter speeds are displayed in the viewfinder.

The lens mount is the Nikon bayonet but only lenses with a meter coupling prong—such as most recent Nikkor lenses—couple with the full aperture metering system. Other lenses must be metered at shooting aperture.

EL Features

1	Stop-down button	9	Film cassette
2	Maximum aperture scale	10	View finder eyepiece
3	3 mm flash contact	11	Focal plane shutter
4	Mirror lock button	12	Film guides
5	Lens release button	13	Sprocketed drive spindle
6	Rewind knob/back release	14	Film take-up spool
7	Battery check button	15	Take-up sprocket
8	Battery check light	16	Camera back

Nikkormat FT2

The Nikkormat FT2 is a 35 mm single-lens reflex camera with eye-level viewing through a fixed pentaprism. Its lenses interchange using the Nikon bayonet system, allowing the use of a vast variety of focal lengths and the fitting of many other accessories. Diaphragm operation is automatic. Shutter speeds from 1/1000 to 1 sec and B are set with the ring round the lens mount; and the shutter is cocked using the film advance lever. The shutter is released either with the button on the top plate, or with the self-timer on the front panel. The reflex mirror returns to the viewing position immediately after each exposure, but may be locked up if needed. A hot shoe contact and a 3 mm (PC) flash terminal on the camera body are synchronised to suit the shutter speed chosen.

The camera is fitted with a CdS exposure meter which reads through whatever lens is fitted to the camera. With a Nikkor lens fitted with a coupling prong, the meter is coupled to the film speed, shutter speed and lens aperture, and readings are taken at full aperture. With other lenses, and non-meter-coupled accessories, the film and shutter speeds remain coupled, but the meter is set to read at the picture-taking aperture by moving the meter coupling pin as far to the right (looking at the camera) as possible. The meter is powered by a 1.5 volt silver oxide battery housed in the camera base.

FT2 Features

1	Shutter release button	16	Depth-of-field scale
2	Frame counter	17	Neck strap lug
3	Film transport lever	18	Self-timer
4	Film plane indicator	19	Lens
5	Flash contact	20	Shutter speed index
6	Viewfinder eyepiece	21	Meter coupling prong
7	Accessory shoe	22	Mirror lock
8	Meter read-out	23	Lens release button
9	Rewind crank	24	Rewind release button
10	Stop-down button	25	Tripod bush
11	Meter coupling pin	26	Film speed scale
12	Aperture setting ring	27	Shutter speed lever
13	Aperture and focus index	28	Film speed lock
14	Focus ring	29	Battery compartment
15	Focus scale		

16

Nikkormat FT2

With the 50 mm $f2$ lens, the Nikkormat FT2 weighs 970 g (2 lb 1 oz). When the 55 mm $f1.2$ lens is fitted, the weight is increased to 1185 g (2 lb 9 oz). The body alone weighs 765 g (1 lb 10 oz) and is 148 mm ($5\frac{13}{16}$ in) wide, 95 mm ($3\frac{3}{4}$ in) high and 54 mm ($2\frac{1}{8}$ in) thick.

The camera uses 35 mm film, either in film manufacturers' cassettes, or in reloadable magazines. It does not use cassettes intended for the Nikon F or F2 cameras. The picture is the standard 24 × 36 mm size. A pressure plate and roller accurately registers the film against the gate.

The lens mount is the Nikon bayonet but only lenses with a meter coupling prong—such as most recent Nikkor lenses—will couple with the full aperture metering system. Other lenses must be metered at shooting aperture.

FT2 Features

1	Shutter speed scale	7	Focal plane shutter
2	Maximum aperture scale	8	Viewfinder eyepiece
3	3 mm flash contact	9	Sprocketed drive spindle
4	Back release catch	10	Film take-up spool
5	Film cassette chamber	11	Film take-up sprocket
6	Film guides	12	Camera back

18

Nikkormat system

Nikkormat cameras are manufactured by Nippon Kogaku KK as a complement to the Nikon cameras. Most of the Nikon accessories, except the interchangeable viewfinders and motor drives, are also suitable for the Nikkormats. All the lenses carry the name Nikkor.

Lenses
Straightforward Nikkor accessory lenses range from 15 to 2000 mm, as well as a series of zoom lenses covering the range 28 mm to 1200 mm, five fisheye lenses from 6 mm to 16 mm for a variety of purposes, a number of specialist lenses for macro work, and two perspective control lenses. Nikon supply a range of all glass filters matched to their lenses, and an enormous range of other accessories to make the Nikkormat an extremely versatile photographic tool.

Viewfinder accessories
A number of accessories alter the viewfinder image: the clip-on focusing telescope which can be hinged out of the way, allows critical focusing of the central part; the right-angle finder, which can be swivelled through 360°, allows you to see in awkward situations, such as low level or microscope work; and the eyepiece correction lenses, in nine dioptre strengths from −5 to +3 can be fitted for spectacle wearers who don't like wearing them for photography.

Close-ups
A major field of photography involves getting extra close to the subject. The Nikon range of equipment includes: close-up lenses; automatic meter coupled and manual extension tubes; bellows units; a simple adapter for fitting the camera to a microscope; macro lenses of 55 and 105 mm focal lengths, and the 200 mm *f*5.6 Medical Nikkor, which has a built-in flash unit. The Bellows PB4 are a particularly sturdy four rail unit with a front panel that may be swung or shifted to give some perspective control and depth-of-field manipulation. The Bellows PB5 are simpler and lighter than PB4 and are photographically their equal except for the front standard movement. Either bellows may be fitted with one of the slide copiers PS4 and PS5.

Other equipment
For more general copying, the repro-copy outfit Model PF-2 provides a firm support for vertical photography. It is built into a wooden case, which folds flat to form a base-board. The camera support arm is fitted with a focusing rail.

Nikon equipment also includes a pistol grip with built-in trigger, which is especially useful with longer focus lenses; a panorama head to allow conjoining pictures to be taken covering up to 360 degrees; and a flash unit with all types of small bulbs.

There are individual cases available for Nikkormat cameras, and for Nikkor lenses. There is also a wide range of leather and plastic compartment cases, designed to hold particular combinations of equipment.

Nikkormat Accessories

A	Bulb flash		
B	Electronic flash	K	Interchangeable lenses
C	Rubber eyecup	L	Extension tubes
D	Correction lenses	M	Microscope adapter
E	Focusing telescope	N	Pistol grip
F	Right-angle finder	O	Slide copiers
G	Reversing ring	P	Bellows attachments
H	Filters	Q	Panorama head
J	Close-up lenses	R	Repro-copy outfit

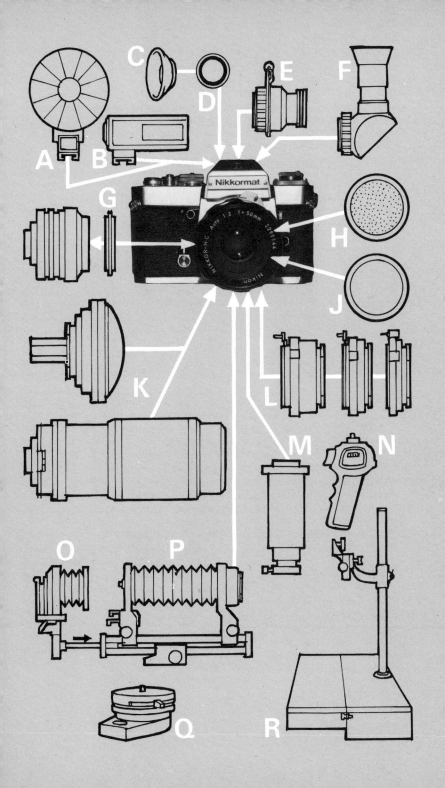

The viewfinder and focusing

Nikkormat cameras have a ground glass viewing screen with a central rangefinder spot. This comprises a split image rangefinder surrounded by a microprism grid. Round this is a plain ground glass collar. To ensure even illumination, a fresnel condenser lens is formed below the rest of the screen. This is just visible as a series of fine concentric rings. On the FT2, the shutter speed set is displayed immediately below the aperture flanked by the next higher and lower speeds in yellow. The meter needle is set on the right of the screen. Metered shutter speeds are displayed on the left-hand side of the EL viewfinder screen. A needle indicates the required speed, and a green band the mechanically set speed. (See p. 32).

The viewfinder image is about life-size with a 55 mm lens, and slightly smaller with a 50 mm lens. Whatever lens (from the whole range) is fitted, the screen shows just slightly less than will be recorded on the film. The difference is to allow a safety margin for transparency mounts and negative carriers. Spectacle wearers will be able to see most of the screen area without moving the camera, but they may find it advisable to fit a rubber eyecup to prevent scratching their glasses on the metal eyepiece surround. When taking pictures, make sure that the whole composition is satisfactory. It is too easy to concentrate on your main subject in the viewfinder and only after processing notice distractions elsewhere in the picture.

Focusing the lens

Looking through your viewfinder you will see that, as you rotate the focusing ring, objects at varying distances away are sharply focused on the screen. To focus on a particular subject, look at the image on the screen and turn the focusing ring back and forward until the image is sharp. Alternatively, you can focus by using the central rangefinder. When the camera is pointed towards an out-of-focus subject, the microprism grid appears to shimmer and vertical lines are broken by the split-image spot. When the subject is exactly in focus the shimmer disappears, the subject is seen clearly and unbroken in the centre. Turn the camera to a vertical position if you want horizontal lines to cross the rangefinder split. The rangefinder is formed from moulded prisms, and is of little use at lens apertures smaller than $f4$ or $f5.6$, when part blacks out.

On the screen or with the rangefinder, it is easiest to focus the camera quickly and accurately at full aperture. Because of the small depth of field (see p. 26), small changes of focus are easily seen on the focusing screen.

To be ready for unexpected action, it is advisable to keep your camera set for a useful zone of sharp focus. For example, with the standard lens focused at 15 ft and set to $f11$, everything from about 10 to 30 feet from the camera will be pin-sharp; and everything from about 8 ft to infinity will be acceptably sharp for 'unrepeatable news' or record shots. Naturally, the shutter speed should be pre-set appropriately for the weather conditions, or the EL set to 'automatic'.

Focusing

TOP

The viewfinder screen

1 Fresnel lens
2 Microprism collar
3 Ground glass collar
4 Split-image rangefinder

BOTTOM

As you focus on a subject, the microprism area comes clear, and the split image exactly continuous.

1 →
2 →
3 ←
4 ←

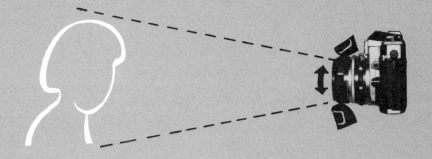

OUT OF FOCUS

IN FOCUS

Exposure controls

A film of a particular sensitivity, or speed (see p. 92), will only produce a satisfactory picture on processing if it has been exposed to the right amount of light.

The intensity of light actually reaching the film is adjusted by altering the aperture in the lens diaphragm, and the length of time it falls on the film is determined by the shutter speed.

Lens aperture

The diaphragm reduces the light rather like drawing curtains across a window, but consists of a number of metal leaves, which form a roughly circular hole of variable size (the limiting aperture). Nikkor camera lenses, and most others, are marked with an aperture scale in f-numbers or relative apertures. These are calculated as the focal length of the lens divided by the diameter of the effective aperture (the area of the light beam striking the front glass which actually passes through the diaphragm at each setting). The f-numbers scale is:

$$1 \quad 1.4 \quad 2 \quad 2.8 \quad 4 \quad 5.6 \quad 8 \quad 11 \quad 16 \quad 22 \quad 32 \quad 45$$

each of which is $\sqrt{2}$ times the one before, and represents half its area. Thus, for example, a lens set to $f4$ passes twice the light of one set to $f5.6$. The ends of the scale vary for different lenses, and often the maximum aperture is intermediate between two of the standard settings. The light reaching the film, from a constantly illuminated subject, is the same at a given f-number for any lens, except when taking close-up photographs (see p. 121).

Most lenses have click stops at each setting on the standard scale, and some also half-way between these. Any lens, however, may be set to intermediate positions between these points if so desired.

Shutter speeds

Almost all modern cameras that have indicated shutter speeds, including all Nikkormats, put them on the scale:

$$1, \quad \tfrac{1}{2}, \quad \tfrac{1}{4}, \quad \tfrac{1}{8}, \quad 1/15, \quad 1/30, \quad 1/60, \quad 1/125, \quad 1/250, \quad 1/500, \quad 1/1000 \text{ sec.}$$

on which each successive speed is half the one before. Thus changing by one speed either halves or doubles the light which falls on the film. Some cameras do not allow all the settings, others allow more, extending the range at one or both ends of the scale. The fractions of a second are indicated by their denominators only, thus 1/250 sec is marked on the Nikkormat shutter speed dials as 250. Intermediate settings cannot be used below 1/250 on the FT2 or at all on the EL. On automatic, however, the EL gives exactly the speed determined by the meter, with no fixed points.

A change from one f-stop to another, or from one marked shutter speed to another is called one *stop*. Thus, to increase an exposure of 1/125 at $f8$ by one stop, the camera must be set either to 1/60 at $f8$ or to 1/125 at $f5.6$. Any particular exposure can be produced in a number of ways; for example: $\tfrac{1}{4}$, $f22$; $\tfrac{1}{8}$, $f16$; 1/15, $f11$; 1/30, $f8$; 1/60, $f5.6$; 1/125, $f4$; 1/250, $f2.8$; 1/500, $f2$ and 1/1000, $f1.4$ all expose the film the same amount, and the choice between them gives the photographer creative control.

Controlling exposure

TOP
Shutter speed and aperture combine

BOTTOM
Closing the diaphragm reduces the light like drawing curtains across a window

24

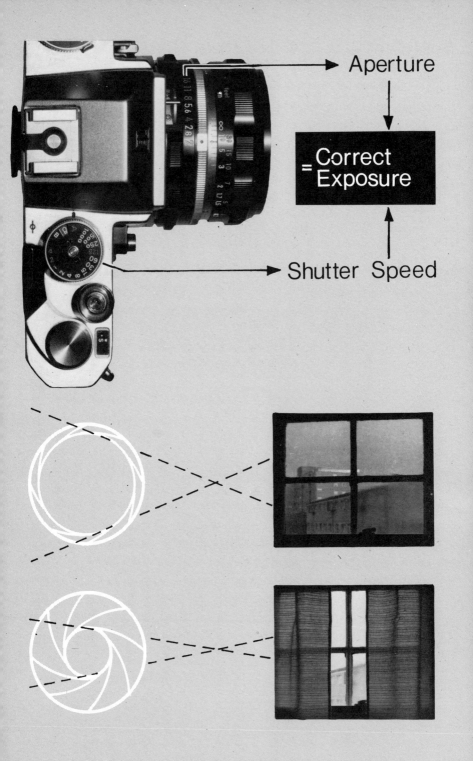

Aperture

= Correct Exposure

Shutter Speed

Aperture and depth of field

Although used primarily to control the exposure (with the shutter speed) the lens aperture has a further effect on the final picture. It determines how much of the subject is recorded sharply. Anything exactly at the focused distance is rendered absolutely sharp, provided there is no camera or subject movement. However, closer objects and those farther away will theoretically be not quite as sharp. In practice, there is always a zone of sharp focus from somewhere in front of the subject to somewhere behind it. This is called the depth of field, and its magnitude is determined by the lens aperture and the focused distance. The larger the aperture (smaller the f-number), the smaller the depth of field for a particular lens, and also the closer the focused distance, the smaller the depth.

It is not actually the f-number, but the effective aperture (see p. 24) which determines the depth of field. Thus, the depth (at any given focused distance) for a 50 mm lens at f5.6 is the same as that for a 200 mm lens at f22. Of course, the depth of field for a 200 mm lens at f5.6 is much smaller.

The depth of field may be seen through the viewfinder if the lens is stopped down to the selected aperture. With automatic lenses you can press the stop down button. On pre-set and other manual lenses, just turn the diaphragm ring. Depth of field may, alternatively, be read from the scale on the lens barrel. When the lens is focused, the limits of sharp focus are indicated on the distance scale by the two marks corresponding to the selected f-number. The lines are colour coded, corresponding to the colour of the f-number markings on the aperture scale. There is not room to engrave marks for all the possible apertures, so some are left out. You have to interpolate between the coloured lines for the white numbered aperture settings. The small red dot indicates the infra-red focusing mark (see p. 46).

Practical effects

A small depth of field may be used to creative purpose—for example to make a sharply focused subject stand out against a soft background. This is achieved by choosing a large lens aperture (e.g. f4 on a 50 mm lens). In other circumstances, as small an aperture as practical (e.g. f16) must be chosen to render as much as possible of the subject sharp. The greatest usable depth is obtained by focusing neither on the foreground subject, nor on the background, but somewhere in between. For distant subjects set the depth-of-field calibration for your chosen aperture against the infinity (∞) mark. The focused distance (see p. 120) is then called the hyperfocal distance for that aperture. The closest sharp focus (indicated by the other calibration the same colour) is half the hyperfocal distance.

Depth of Field

TOP
You can see the extent of sharp focus on the lens scale. The coloured lines correspond with the same coloured f numbers on the scale. Typical colours are shown opposite.

BOTTOM
You can see the actual sharpness on the viewing screen by stopping down the lens. Use the stop-down button for automatic lenses.

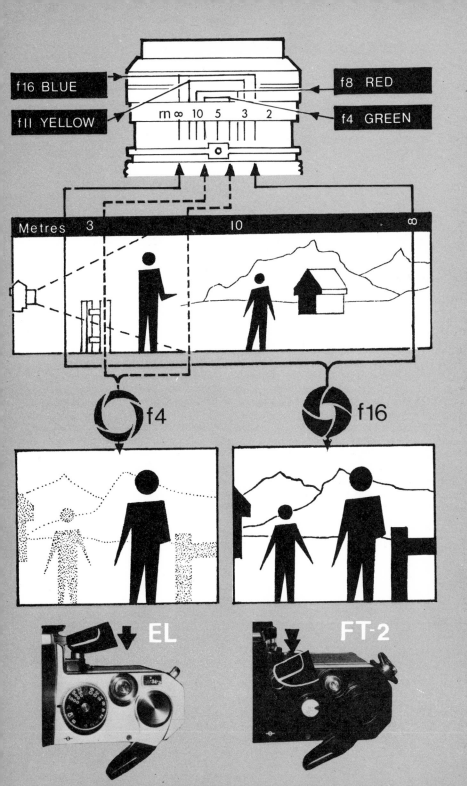

Shutter speed and function

The shutter is cocked when the film is wound on, and the shutter speed may be set either before or after this operation.

This is done on the EL by turning the dial on the camera top so that the required value is next to the black mark beside the pentaprism housing. The speed set is also indicated by the green bar on the scale to the left of the viewfinder image. The speeds in black on the scale or white on the dial are the denominators of fractions of a second; thus 60 refers to 1/60 sec, 250 to 1/250 sec and so on; the figures in red on the scale and orange on the dial indicate 1, 2 and 4 seconds. (The red 125 indicates the maximum shutter speed usable with electronic flash.) Do not select intermediate speed settings manually. If the dial is set to 'A', the camera will choose its shutter speeds automatically. The green bar stays at the 'A' position at the top of the shutter speed scale. The shutter speed is altered by changing the lens aperture and indicated by the viewfinder needle. The speed dial can be moved from the automatic position only when the lock button at its centre is pressed. If the battery is not up to power (see p. 54) shutter speeds, whether set manually or automatically may be erratic, and cannot be relied on. With the battery removed or completely flat, the camera will give 1/90 sec wherever the dial is set.

On the FT2, the shutter speed is set by rotating the ring round the lens mount until the required speed is shown against the black dot above and to the right (the speeds are all fractions of a second). There is a lever below and to the left for turning the ring. Do not set intermediate speeds below 1/250 sec.

Effects
The shutter speed determines the time that the light from the subject is focused on the film. If the image moves significantly during the exposure time, the picture will be blurred. Image movement is caused by subject movement or by camera movement (camera shake). To record them sharply, fast moving subjects, such as athletes or railway trains, need fast shutter speeds (1/500 or 1/1000 sec); moderately moving subjects such as groups of people or townscapes, need moderate shutter speeds (1/60 to 1/250 sec), whereas still subjects can be photographed at any shutter speed—provided the camera does not move. If you hold the camera very steadily (see p. 38) you will probably be able to get acceptably sharp pictures of relatively immobile subjects at 1/30 sec, with the standard lens, but it is easier to get them at faster speeds. Below 1/30 sec some form of support is needed, as it is at higher speeds with longer focus lenses.

To give an impression of movement, a relatively slow shutter speed may be used so that a blurred image is formed as the subject passes the static camera. Another technique is to follow the movement by swinging the camera (panning) so that the subject appears sharp against a blurred background. With high-speed subjects, try 1/60 or 1/125 as a start.

Nikkormat cameras have vertically running focal plane shutters. At fast shutter speeds the film is exposed sequentially as the gap passes across it. At 1/125 sec or slower, all the film area is simultaneously uncovered for part of the exposure. This is essential for flash pictures except when using special bulbs (see p. 52).

Shutter speeds and movement
TOP
Any speed can record a still life sharply.

MIDDLE
Moderate speeds give blurred pictures of moving subjects
BOTTOM
Fast speeds 'freeze' motion.

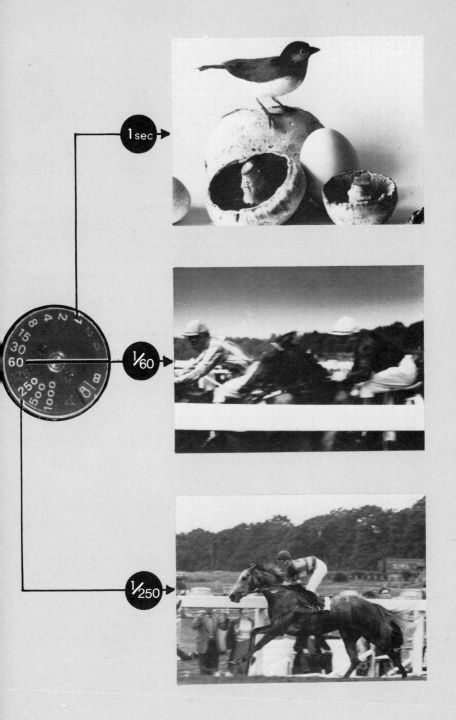

Measuring exposure

Nikkormat cameras measure the light reflected from the subject. In fact, the meter measures the light intensity on the viewing screen with a degree of centre weighting. Most normal subjects average out (integrate) to a mid grey, and the meters are calibrated to produce a result which matches this. Even if the subject does not integrate to a mid tone, the meter reading will still produce a picture which does. Thus, the meter's recommendation for any subject will produce a mid-tone result, whether the subject be a sunlit white-washed wall, or the inside of an unlit coal-mine.

For most normal subjects, lit from somewhere behind the camera, following the meter's recommendation will give an ideal exposure; but where the subject includes large unusually lit areas, you should adjust the exposure accordingly. The centre-weighted Nikkormat meters give more prominence to tones falling in the centre of the field, and thus will give accurate readings even if parts of the edges of the view are unusually lit, but in strongly contrasting situations some compensations must be made. The general rule is to give less exposure for subjects against a dark background and more for those against a light one. When the subject is back-lit, it usually needs about two stops more exposure than a meter reading of the whole scene recommends.

Selective metering

One method of obtaining an alternative reading is to meter only part of the subject—for example, a person's face when taking an against-the-light portrait. Focus the camera so that the chosen part fills the viewing screen (for this you will have to go closer, or use a longer focus lens). Take your meter reading, and use the recommended exposure for your picture. Another method is to take a meter reading from a standard test object, lit in exactly the same way as your subject. The professionally recommended standard is an 18 per cent grey card, which closely approximates the average reflectance of a normal scene. A more convenient standard is the palm of your hand. A few test frames will show you how best to modify readings taken from your chosen standard. When using the EL on automatic, you can hold an exposure setting with the memory lock (see p. 32).

No need to meter every shot

When you are taking a number of similar shots on one location with the FT2, it is usually best to take meter readings before you start shooting, set your camera, and not to alter the exposure again unless there is a great change in the light level. Only when shooting colour transparencies is the exposure likely to be critical enough to warrant camera setting changes under normal lighting conditions, and even then they will usually be unnecessary. Unless you are shooting in difficult conditions, you can leave the EL set to automatic, thus removing the need to pay any attention to exposure. If you set a higher or lower film speed than normal, this will give you consistent under- or over-exposure should the circumstances require it (either by doubling or halving the ASA setting alters the exposure by 1 stop).

Measuring exposure

TOP

Move the camera to avoid large brightly lit areas when metering.

BOTTOM

1   Backlit subjects may be underexposed.
2   Meter from important subject area.
3   Move back with that exposure for correct picture.

Operating the EL Exposure meter

The EL meter operates whether or not the shutter dial is set to 'A' (automatic). The meter must be set for the sensitivity (speed) of the film being used by pressing in the catch, and turning the milled ring surrounding the re-wind knob until the red index mark is against the correct ASA figure (between 25 and 1600). The values of the dots between the numerical calibrations are given opposite.

Coupled lenses

When the camera is fitted directly with a lens with diaphragm coupling prong, meter readings are taken at full aperture unless the lens has deliberately been fitted without the prong coupled. When fitting a meter-coupled lens, you must set the meter for maximum aperture (see p. 56).

Pulling out the film transport lever to reveal the red dot switches on the meter (and unlocks the shutter release button). The shutter speed to suit the film speed, lens aperture and prevailing light is then indicated by the needle on the left-hand side of the viewfinder screen. The camera should be focused on the subject to take a reading (see p. 30).

The lens aperture ring may then be adjusted to give the required combination of aperture and shutter speed—the shutter speed indication alters as the aperture is changed. If the shutter speed knob is set to 'A', the camera automatically gives the indicated shutter speed; otherwise, the speed must be mechanically set to match the green bar to the needle in the viewfinder (but intermediate speeds should not be selected manually). This may be done by altering either or both the shutter speed and aperture controls, remembering that both can influence the final picture. When the camera is set to automatic operation, the green bar indicates 'A' at the top of the scale.

Non-coupled lenses

If the camera is fitted with a lens without a diaphragm coupling prong—or if the lens is mounted on non-coupling close-up accessories such as bellows, extension tubes or microscope adapter—you must use stop-down metering (see p. 36).

Memory lock

By pressing the memory lock lever towards the lens you can hold an exposure setting until you release the lever. If you want, for example, to use an exposure based on a meter reading from a particular subject area (see p. 30) the memory lock will hold it for you. Although the exposure time is locked, the meter needle continues to vary with the light reaching the lens. The lever may be held in for as many exposures as required; but if you want to take a whole series of pictures not based on the overall lighting, you can either set the shutter speed and aperture manually or you can influence the automatically set exposures by altering the film speed setting. Doubling the film speed will give you exactly one stop under-exposure, and halving it one stop over-exposure compared to the normally metered settings. Remember to put the setting back to normal afterwards.

Always switch the meter off after use. Otherwise battery life may be reduced.

Metering with the Nikkormat EL

1 Set film speed.	5 Select aperture to give:
2 Switch on meter.	6 Suitable shutter speed/or:
3 Set to automatic/or:	6a Match needle to green bar.
3a Select shutter speed.	7 Memory lock holds exposure on
4 Focus on subject.	auto.

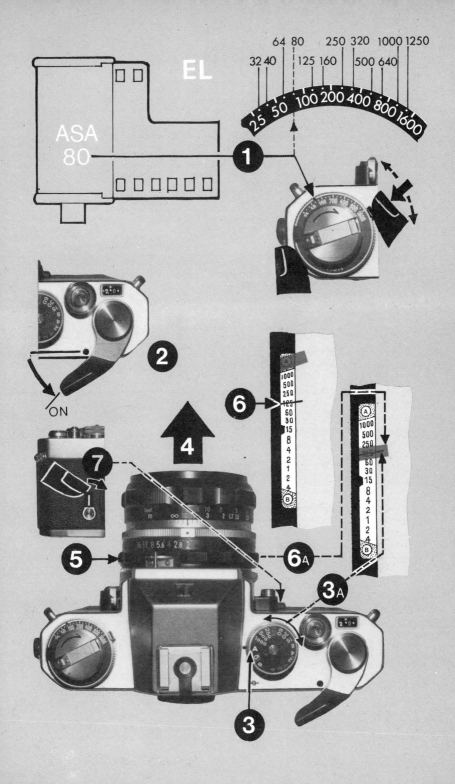

Operating the FT2 exposure meter

To obtain a correct reading, the meter must be set for the correct film speed (see p. 91). This is done by pulling out the tip of the shutter speed knob, and two-pronged index below the lens until the correct ASA reading shows against the notch in the centre of the cut-out. The dots between the numerical calibrations indicate speeds as shown in the table opposite.

The meter is switched on by pulling out the film advance lever until the red dot is revealed. The lever will remain in that position until it is pushed back. The exposure is then selected by focusing the camera on the subject—or that part of it from which you wish to meter—and adjusting the shutter speed and aperture controls until the meter needle is centred in its cut-out. Under- and over-exposure are indicated by the — and + marks above and below the cut-out.

Measuring procedure

The normal procedure is to preselect a suitable shutter speed, focus the camera on the subject and centre the meter needle by moving the aperture setting ring. The camera is then set to give the metered exposure. If you wish to shoot at a particular aperture, you may preselect the aperture and centre the needle with the shutter speed ring. The ring should not, however, be set to any position between the marked speeds below 1/250 sec. A meter reading in the B setting indicates a measured exposure of 2 seconds.

The needle just touches the lower edge of the square frame when over-exposing by 1 stop, and the upper edge when underexposing by 1 stop. Any further deviation from recommendation, and the needle moves to its rest position either below or above the cut-out. The degree of over- or under-exposure cannot be relied on beyond one stop.

The meter coupling range (i.e. the range of shutter speeds and apertures at which it will work) varies with the film speed set and the lens used. With the 50 mm f1.4 lens and a 100 ASA film speed, the range extends from $\frac{1}{4}$ sec at f1.4 to 1/1000 sec at f11 (or equivalent combination). Outside the coupling range the meter switches off, the needle returning to its rest position above the under exposure mark.

Metering with the Nikkormat FT2

1   Set film speed.
2   Switch on meter.
3   Select shutter speed.
4   Focus on subject.
5   Alter lens aperture to:
6   Centre needle or:
7   Alter shutter speed to centre it.

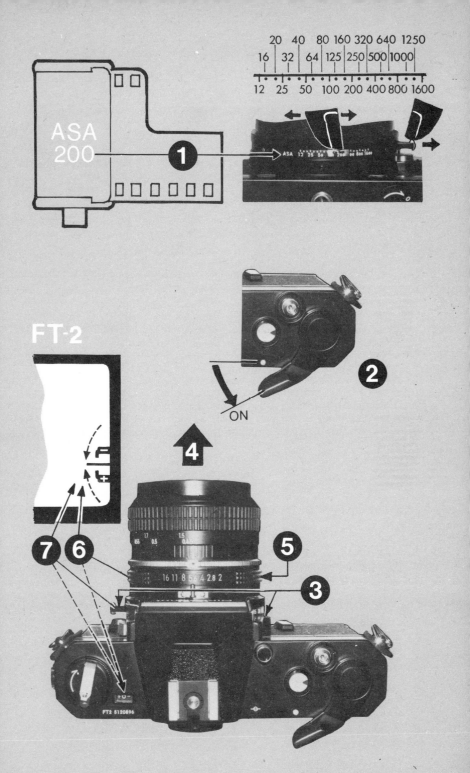

Stop-down metering

When the camera is fitted with a non-meter-coupled lens or behind-the-lens accessory, meter readings are made at the picture-taking aperture. The meter is set to the stop-down mode by moving the coupling pin as far to the right as possible. With automatic lenses or accessories, the stop-down button must be pressed in before metering. This stops the lens down to its set aperture, but it remains stopped down only until the button is released. Note that the film must not be wound on while the stop-down button is depressed. If the stop-down button is used with a meter-coupled lens, the meter gives an inaccurate reading. With pre-set and other manual lenses, or with non-automatic accessories, the stop-down button need not be used, as the diaphragm is set directly with its ring.

EL
Once the meter is switched on and the lens diaphragm can be closed down with its setting ring, metering can proceed. Focus the camera on the subject (or that part from which readings are to be taken). On the EL, the meter needle then registers the required shutter speed and sets it if the shutter dial is set to 'A'; otherwise, match the green pointer to the needle by altering the shutter speed and aperture as required. When shooting with a non-meter-coupled automatic diaphragm lens in the automatic mode, you must stop down manually before releasing the shutter for each exposure, otherwise the camera sets the shutter speed appropriate to the full aperture of the lens in use.

FT2
On the FT2, simply centre the meter needle in the cut-out by adjusting the aperture and shutter speed dials. It is usual to preselect a shutter speed and set the exposure by altering the aperture, but the reverse procedure may be used when necessary. Make sure, however, that the shutter speed dial is not set to a position between the marked speeds below 1/250 sec. If so desired, for viewing or focusing, automatic lenses may be returned to full aperture by releasing the stop-down button after metering.

Stop-down metering
TOP
Nikkormat EL

A *Automatic exposure with automatic diaphragm lenses.*

1 Move meter pin fully.	4 Press stop-down button.
2 Mount lens or accessory.	5 Alter aperture to:
3 Switch on.	6 Select suitable shutter speed.

B *Manual exposure with manual diaphragm operation.*

1 Move meter pin fully.	4 Select shutter speed to:
2 Mount lens or accessory.	5 Match green bar.
3 Switch on meter.	Alter aperture if speed is unsuitable.

BOTTOM
Nikkormat FT2

1 Move meter pin fully.	4 Stop down automatic lens.
2 Mount lens or accessory.	5 Adjust shutter speed and
3 Switch on meter.	aperture to centre needle.

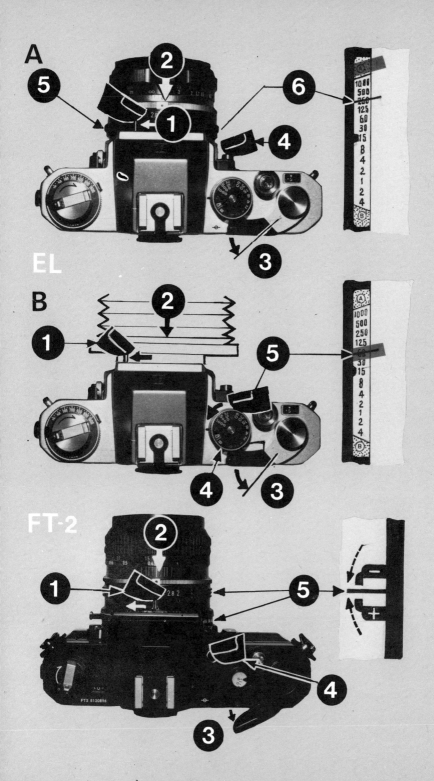

A

EL

B

FT-2

Holding the camera

The way you hold your camera can influence the quality of your pictures. If the camera moves, even minutely, while the shutter is open, the picture will not have quite the absolute sharpness you should expect from a good quality instrument. Camera shake, as such movement is called, is one of the most common causes of lack of definition, even in pictures taken by experienced photographers. The effect is not necessarily the serious multiple image effect produced when a beginner waves around a camera while using a long shutter speed, it may just be a slight thickening of lines and smudging of fine detail.

Naturally the danger of camera shake is greatest at long (slow) shutter speeds, as is the magnitude of its effects. However, image blur caused by movement is possible at all shutter speeds, and the risk is proportionately greater the longer the focal length of the lens in use.

The only way to be absolutely sure of eliminating movement is to support the camera firmly—on a tripod or other solid object—and use a cable release or the self-timer (see pages 46, 48) to release the shutter. This is, of course, impractical in many situations; but when hand-holding, you should try to find a firm support for yourself or the camera. For example you may be able to lean against a wall or a lamp-post, or perhaps sit or lie on the ground.

Stand comfortably
Whether or not you use any additional bracing, make sure that you are in a comfortable and stable position. Generally, the steadiest unsupported stance is that pictured opposite, with the weight evenly distributed on slightly parted legs. Your elbows should be kept well in to your sides, and the camera held firmly against your face with both hands.

While the right hand should be in a comfortable position to operate the shutter release and wind on the film, the left hand operates the focusing aperture selection rings and the lens. In general, at the instant of picture-taking, this hand should hold the camera more tightly than the right. Convenient grips for both horizontal and vertical pictures are shown opposite. Some photographers prefer to hold the camera the other way up for vertical photos, using their right thumb to release the shutter.

Finally, don't hold the camera too tightly, or your fingers will soon get fatigued and start to shake; and, when the right moment comes, hold your breath and squeeze the release button very gently to take the picture.

Holding your Nikkormat

Stand in a steady stance and squeeze the shutter release gently to avoid camera shake.

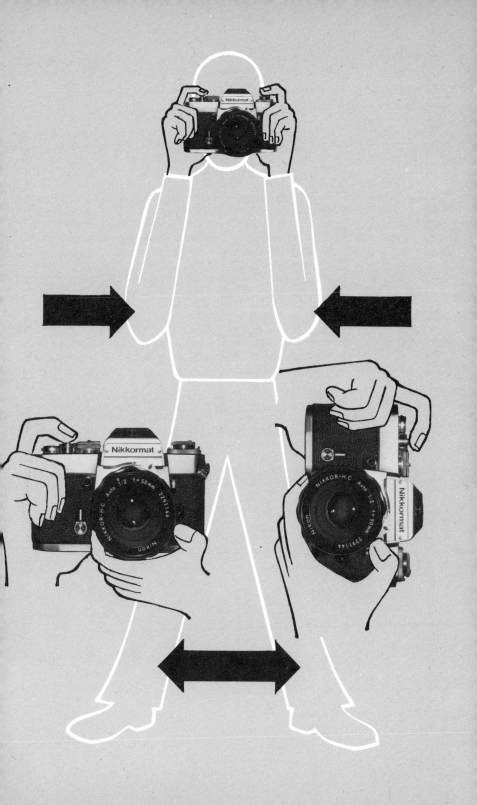

Loading

Film is loaded into the back of Nikkormat cameras either in film manufacturers' cassettes, or in reloadable cassettes. The operation should be carried out in the shade—if necessary turn your back to the sun. If you already have a film in the camera, this must be rewound before you can load in the next one (see p. 44).

The loading sequence is similar whichever camera you use: Unlock the back by releasing the catch and pulling up the rewind knob on the EL, or by pulling down the back release on the FT2. Hinge open the back cover. Pull up the rewind knob (on the FT2), and place the EL cassette in the film chamber. Push the rewind knob back in, turning it slightly to engage the cassette spindle. Push the end of the film leader into one of the slots on the take-up spool, making sure that it is held by the small tooth above the lower flange.

Turn the take-up spool about one turn towards the shutter to ensure that the film is securely engaged. Wind on the film leader by turning the film transport lever, releasing the shutter if necessary. Make sure that the drive spindle sprockets engage the perforations top and bottom of the film, and that it lies flat between the outer film guides. Turn the rewind knob *gently* in the direction of the arrow to take up any slack in the film. Close the camera back, pressing firmly until it clicks.

To wind on the film exposed to the light during loading, operate the film transport lever twice, releasing the shutter after each stroke. Watch the rewind knob as you wind on, it should turn counter-clockwise to show that the film is being wound. The frame counter should now indicate '0'. Wind on a third stroke, and the frame counter should now indicate 1, showing that the camera is ready for the first exposure on the film.

Set the film's speed in the cut-out on the shutter speed ring of the FT2, or round the rewind knob of the EL (see pp. 32, 34). The dial is calibrated in ASA speeds.

Loading the Nikkormat

1	Pull up rewind knob.	7	Operate transport lever.
1A	Pull down catch (FT2).	8	Make sure sprockets engage.
2	Open back.	9	Take up slack in cassette.
3	Insert cassette.	10	Close back.
4	Push back rewind knob.	11	Operate transport lever three
5	Insert leader in slot.		times.
6	Wind spool to take up slack.	12	Set film speed.

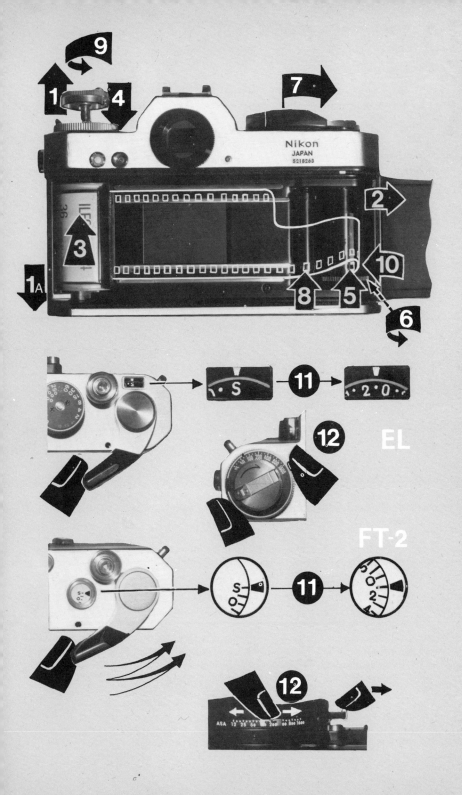

EL

FT-2

Shooting

When the camera is loaded, and the film speed set, switch on the meter (this also unlocks the shutter release on the EL), make sure that the film has been wound on, take off the lens cap and you are ready to make the first exposure. The metering procedure differs on the two models.

Shooting with the EL

Point the camera at your subject and focus with the ring. Adjust the lens aperture ring until the meter needle indicates the shutter speed you require. Remember that aperture and shutter speed both influence the final picture (see pp. 26, 28).

You may otherwise set the shutter speed manually, and select the aperture by matching the meter needle to the green bar on the viewfinder scale. With a non-meter-coupled lens, you must meter with the lens stopped down. Remember that manual lenses must be stopped down before each exposure, and so must automatic diaphragm lenses when shooting in the automatic mode.

Shooting with the FT2

Preselect either a shutter speed or a lens aperture. Compose your picture in the viewfinder, and focus on your main subject with the ring. Now alter either the aperture ring or the shutter speed dial until the meter needle follower is centred on the needle. (Remember that aperture and shutter speed both influence the final picture.) This gives you optimum exposure for a normal subject; if the subject differs from the usual contrast range you may need to modify the exposure (see p. 30).

To take your meter reading with a non-meter-coupled lens, preselect either a shutter speed or an aperture and having focused your picture with the ring stop down the lens diaphragm to the setting on the aperture ring (using the stop-down switch with automatic lenses), and alter the aperture ring or the shutter speed dial until the follower is centred on the meter needle. Automatic lenses may be allowed to open up again, if desired.

Taking the picture

The rest of the procedure is the same for either camera. Check in the viewfinder that you have exactly the picture you want, hold the camera very still (see p. 38), hold your breath and gently squeeze the shutter release button to take the picture. Wind on the film ready for the next picture.

If you don't intend to take any more pictures immediately, switch off the meter thus saving any drain on the battery, and lock the shutter release button on the EL. Note that the battery in the EL will go flat quite quickly if the meter is left switched on, even with the lens cap in place.

Shooting procedure

TOP
Nikkormat EL.
1   Switch on meter.
2   Remove lens cap.
3   Focus on subject.
4   Alter lens aperture to:
5   Choose suitable shutter speed.

BOTTOM
Nikkormat FT2.
1   Switch on meter.
2   Remove lens cap.
3   Focus on subject.
4   Set shutter speed.
5   Alter lens aperture to:
6   Centre needle.

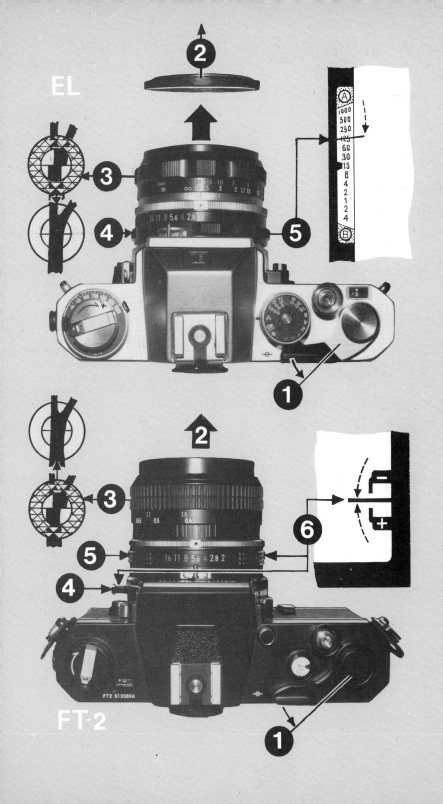

EL

FT·2

Unloading and multiple exposures

Although the frame counter should warn you, you will probably discover the end of the film by a sudden tightening of the film transport lever. Do not force the lever to try to get one more exposure on the film. Even if you are sure you haven't finished the film, it is not worth using force; unload the camera and, if you must, check the cassette later in the darkroom. You may in any case want to take out an unfinished cassette, so that you can load a different type of film.

To unload the camera, depress the film rewind release button, which disengages the film transport mechanism. Lift up the film rewind crank, and wind the film gently back into the cassette—clockwise, in the direction of the arrow. When the film is almost all in the cassette, you will feel a slightly greater resistance; then the leader will pull free from the take-up spool and the rewind crank will turn more freely. If you want to keep the leader outside the cassette so that you can reload it, or to make it easier to load a tank; stop winding at this stage. If you have no reason to use the leader again, wind the film right into the cassette by turning the crank two or three more times. This ensures that you won't reload used films into the camera by mistake. Always label a part-used cassette clearly with the number of exposures used. When you reload it make exposures at a fast shutter speed with the lens cap firmly in place and the viewfinder blocked, until the frame counter reads two more than the number used. This allows a safety margin for differences in loading.

When the film has been rewound you may then open the camera back and take out the cassette. The rewind button will return to its normal position when you next operate the transport lever. If you are not reloading immediately, close the back and push back the knob.

Always have films processed as soon as practicable after unloading the camera. If you must keep them, store unprocessed colour films in a cool, dry place.

Making multiple exposures

Multiple exposures can be achieved with a certain amount of dexterity. First, take up any slack in the film cassette by turning the rewind knob as if to rewind the film and hold it; then hold in the rewind release button while operating the film advance lever. The film will probably remain in the same place.

Unloading

1 Press rewind release button.
2 Rewind film.
3 Open camera back.
3A Nikkormat FT2 catch.
4 Remove cassette.
5 Close camera back.

Making multiple exposures

1 Make first exposure.
2 Take up slack in cassette and hold.
3 Press and hold rewind release button.
4 Operate film transport lever.
5 Make second exposure.

44

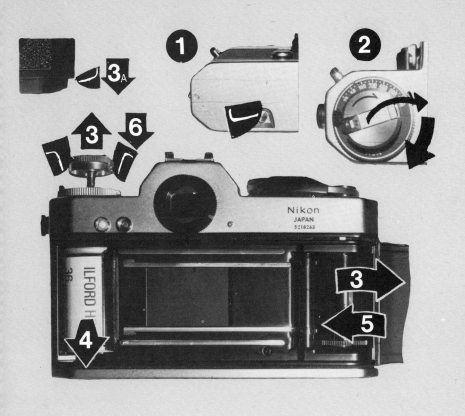

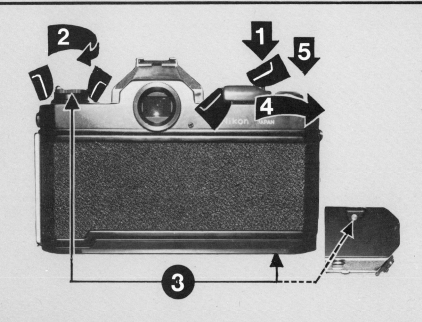

Small features

Self-timer
A self-timer is fitted to the Nikkormat cameras. It is set with the small lever to the left of the lens, which is pushed down in counter-clockwise direction (looking at the front of the camera). When the shutter release button is pressed, the timer lever returns slowly to the upright position, where it releases the shutter (if it is cocked), after a delay of about 10 seconds. If the shutter has not been cocked, the lever will not move. It will operate in the normal way once the shutter is cocked (by operating the film transport lever). The self-timer cannot be over-ridden, and once set, the delay will occur when next the shutter is released. Once the timer is set, the lever on the EL is free to be used for exposure locking purposes, but occasions when this function would be combined with delayed release are hard to imagine.

One use for the self-timer is in taking self-portraits. For this, set up the camera on a firm support, focused on your intended position; set the shutter speed and lens aperture to give the desired exposure, or use the EL on automatic; turn the self-timer lever down and then release it. Use the delay to get into position in front of the lens. Another use is when taking pictures requiring a long exposure. If you have no cable release, you can set the camera on a tripod or other firm support and allow the self-timer to trip the shutter. This avoids the danger of introducing camera shake when pressing the shutter release button.

Mirror lock
The small switch to the right-hand side of the lens mount, above the lens release button raises the reflex mirror. On the EL, the switch hinges up to raise the mirror, and on the FT2 it slides down. Raising the mirror is essential when using some older extremely wide angle lenses (up to 21 mm) and the Fisheye Nikkor 6 mm f5.6 and OP Fisheye Nikkor 10 mm f5.6 lenses which are set so far back that they would foul the mirror in normal operation. These lenses are used with a separate viewfinder. The mirror may also be locked up to make absolutely certain that no vibrations mar long exposures.

Infra-red focusing mark
Infra-red rays and visible rays are brought to focus at different distances from the lens. When using infra-red sensitive film, particularly with an infra-red filter or an infra-red flash, the focused distance should be set against the small red dot in the depth of field scale on the lens (or a red line on some zoom lenses). The procedure is either to set the measured subject distance on the dot, or to focus the visible light image on the screen, and then to move the figure set against the main white or black index to the infra-red index.

Film plane indicator
The position of the film plane—which may be needed for measurements when setting up close-up situations—is shown by the -θ- mark engraved in red on the camera top plate.

A   Self-timer
B   Mirror lock
C   Focusing mark

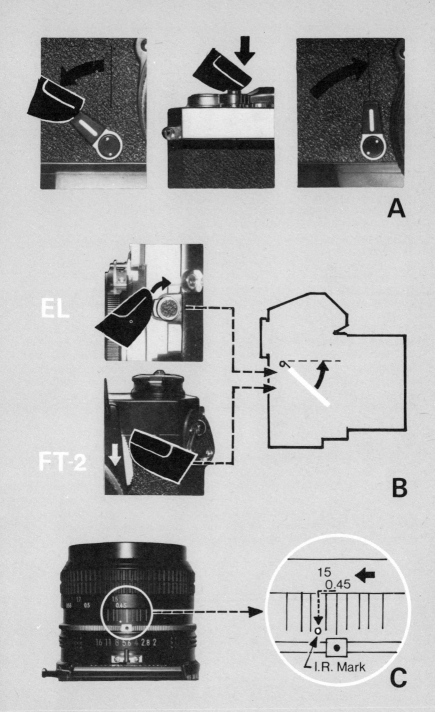

A

EL

FT-2

B

15
0.45

I.R. Mark

C

Cases and other accessories

Cable release
When your camera is mounted on a tripod or other support, you can further guard against camera shake by using a flexible cable release. Nikkormat cameras can be fitted with the commonly available releases which screw into the shutter release button, or the special Nikon type, which screw to the shutter button surround. Whichever type you use, the shutter is released by pressing on the protruding end (unless the release button on the EL is locked). For long time exposures, many cable releases have locking screws which can hold the shutter open (if it is set on B) until they are unscrewed again.

Soft shutter release
A tubular accessory can be screwed over the camera's button. It provides a larger, higher and softer button for more comfortable photography.

Ever-ready case
Hard cases are available for both the EL and the FT2. The camera is fitted to the case by the knurled screw in its base. This incorporates a tripod bush for use if necessary. The front (hinged) portion of the case may be removed if required leaving the rest of the case to prevent the camera body getting scratched.

Other cases
Nikon supply a range of leather and leatherette holdall cases designed especially to carry particular combinations of cameras and equipment. Similarly, there is a range of leather, leatherette, hard plastic or wood lens cases. Thus you can get storage and carrying cases as you need. If you intend to travel much with a selection of equipment, you would be well advised to consider a suitable case (or cases) to reduce the possibility of damage or surface wear to your cameras.

Caps
Nikon supply caps for the front and back of all Nikkor lenses. They also supply camera body caps, so that direct light can be kept out when no lens is mounted. The white plastic cap supplied with the body is only for packing, and is not recommended for continual use. It is advisable to use the appropriate lens or body caps whenever equipment is not in immediate use. The lens caps are important for preventing scratches when lenses are carried loose in a gadget bag. A body cap is particularly important if you store or carry the camera without a lens. It is extremely difficult to remove dirt from the mirror housing, and any abrasive particles may damage the mechanism.

Cases
A Ever ready case.
B Leather compartment case.
C Wooden long focus lens and camera case.
D Plastic lens case.
E Leather lens cases.
F Soft leather lens pouch.

Accessories
G Locking release.
H Soft shutter release.
J Front lens cap.
K Rear lens cap.

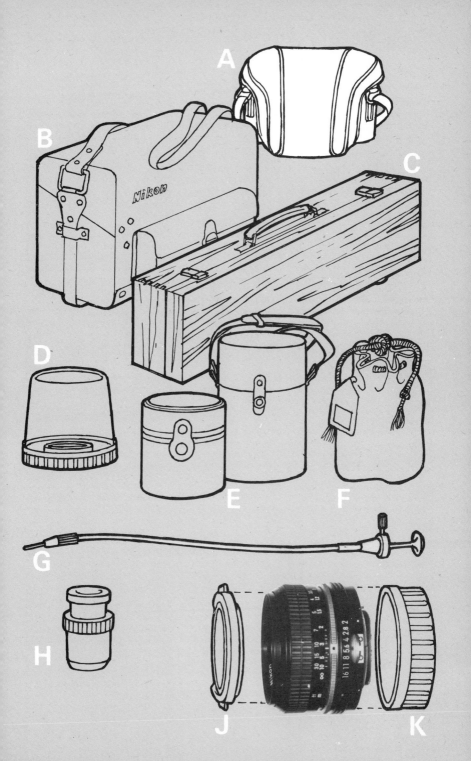

Lens hoods and viewfinder accessories

Lens hoods

Lens hoods (or lens shades) are tubular fittings used to prevent off-angle light striking the front lens element and causing unwanted flare. Nikon manufacture four types—screw-in, snap-on, slip-on and soft (screw-in) rubber hoods. The snap-on hoods can be reversed on the lens for storage and the soft-rubber hoods can be folded back over the lens. It is advisable to use a lens hood whenever there is a strong light-source close to, but not within, the picture area, especially when using a front-mounted filter. Some lenses have built-in extendable hoods, others are supplied with special hoods, and for yet others you can buy hoods that screw on the filter threads. Not only must hoods fit the lens—in the current Nikkor range all standard lenses and most commonly used lenses up to 135 mm have 52 mm filter mounts—but they must suit the lens angle. For example, if you use a hood designed for a 135 mm lens on a standard lens your pictures will show vignetting (darkening or cut-off) in the corners; conversely, the standard lens hood will not be very efficient on the 135 mm lens.

Focusing Magnifier

For critical focusing, especially useful in close-up work, the Eyepiece Magnifier can be screwed onto the eyepiece frame. You can then see the centre of the screen at a choice of two magnifications and thus focus your subject with great accuracy. The magnifier may be hinged out of the way to allow full screen viewing. It has adjustment for eyesight correction from −5 to +1 dioptres.

Right Angle Finder

The Right Angle Viewing Attachment also screws into the eyepiece frame. It has dioptric adjustment by rotating its eyepiece, and allows the screen to be viewed at right angles from above or below the camera from either side or from any position in between. This may be convenient, or even essential, when shooting in confined spaces, from low angles, or with the camera fitted to ancillary equipment such as a microscope. The finder shows a laterally reversed image of the camera screen and the meter needle of the FT2 thus appears on the left-hand side, and the scale of the EL on the right.

Eyesight correction

The Eyepiece Correction Lenses are designed to correct the eyepiece for near- or far-sighted persons who do not like viewing through their glasses. The lenses, made in nine dioptre strengths from −5 to +3 are mounted in circular holders which screw into the eyepiece frame as replacements for the existing eyepiece. The figures quoted are the effective dioptre strengths of the combination of correction lens and viewfinder optics. Some people with a restricted focusing range may find that a slight positive correction to the eyepiece will allow them to focus the screen clearly with their 'distance' glasses, which could otherwise prove difficult. Naturally, the lenses cannot correct for non-spherical sight distortions (astigmatism), and sufferers should have eyepiece lenses ground by a competent optician if they wish to dispense with their glasses while taking photographs.

Accessories

A Lens hood in use.
B Lens hood reversed for storage.
C Right Angle Viewing Attachment swivels to either side.

D Eyepiece Magnifier can be hinged out of the way.
E Correction lenses screw into eyepiece after glass is removed.

A

B

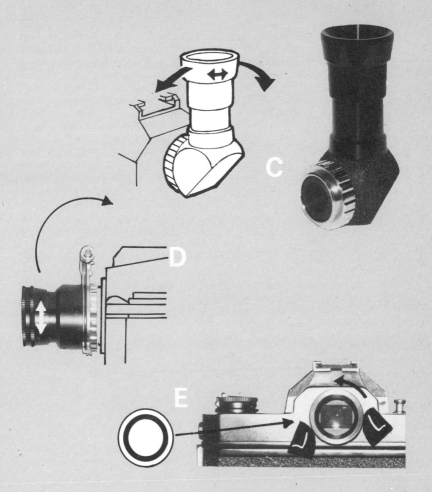

C

D

E

Flash synchronisation

The Nikkormats have a 3 mm coaxial (PC) flash terminal on the side of the body below the rewind knob and a 'hot shoe' contact on top of the prism. You can use a flashgun either with a contact in its base, or with a synchronising lead. The 3 mm sockets are fitted with screw-in covers, and you can use as screw-in lead.

The hot shoe mounting allows the use of a cordless shoe-mounting electronic flash unit, and may also be used as a normal accessory shoe. Some metal-footed flash guns may discharge by shorting across the terminals while their synchronising cord is plugged into the 3 mm socket. A temporary remedy for this is to cover the hot shoe with plastic tape. A better solution is to use a separate shoe on a flash bracket.

On the FT2, both contacts are synchronised for M, and FP class flashbulbs at shutter speeds above 1/125 sec, and X-synchronised at speeds of 1/125 sec and longer.

On the EL, the type of synchronisation is determined by the switch in the shutter setting dial, which may be set either to Ω for bulbs (M) or to $\frac{1}{2}$ for electronic flash (X), by raising its rim and rotating it until the symbol appears in the cut-out.

Shutter speeds

However the unit is connected, flash pictures will be correctly exposed only at certain shutter speeds, depending on the type of flash. This is because at shutter speeds above 1/125 sec. the film is exposed through a moving slit (see p. 28) and will only be evenly illuminated if the light source remains constant for its entire travel. The one flash source that truly fulfils this condition is the focal plane (Class FP) flashbulb. FP bulbs are large and expensive, but there is no alternative for critical work in conditions where the ambient light is too high to use a shutter speed as slow as 1/60 sec. On the M setting the EL fires the flashbulb a few microseconds before the shutter blinds begin their travel, so that the bulb's light output can build up to the constant level needed for even exposure. This happens if the FT2 is set to shutter speeds greater than 1/125 sec.

Depending on the manufacturing tolerances in your camera, and in the flashbulbs, you usually get acceptable pictures using ordinary (M or MF) bulbs with M synchronisation at any speed on the EL. The synchronisation automatically changes with the FT2 shutter speed so you cannot use any sort of flashbulb at 1/60 or 1/125 sec. MF class bulbs should always be used at 1/30 sec or slower on the FT2.

As the duration of an electronic flash is very short (often less than 1/1000 sec), and the build up time is virtually nil, X-synchronisation fires the flash when the shutter is fully open. However, electronic flash can be used only at shutter speeds slow enough for the whole film to be exposed simultaneously. The fastest speed at which it can be used is 1/125 sec, which is marked in red on the shutter speed dial. Pictures taken at higher shutter speeds will be only partly exposed. If an electronic flash unit is used (accidentally) on the M (Ω) setting, none of the flash will reach the film, since it will be fired before the shutter begins to open.

Flash connection

TOP
Flash may be fired through its base contact (A) or its lead B.

MIDDLE
The EL must be set to Ω for flashbulbs or $\frac{1}{2}$ for electronic. Synchronisation is possible at all speeds shown in diagram.

BOTTOM
The FT2 synchronisation is set with the shutter speed. Up to 1/125 sec it is X-synchronised, above 1/125, M-synchronised. The table shows the usable combinations of shutter speed and flash type.

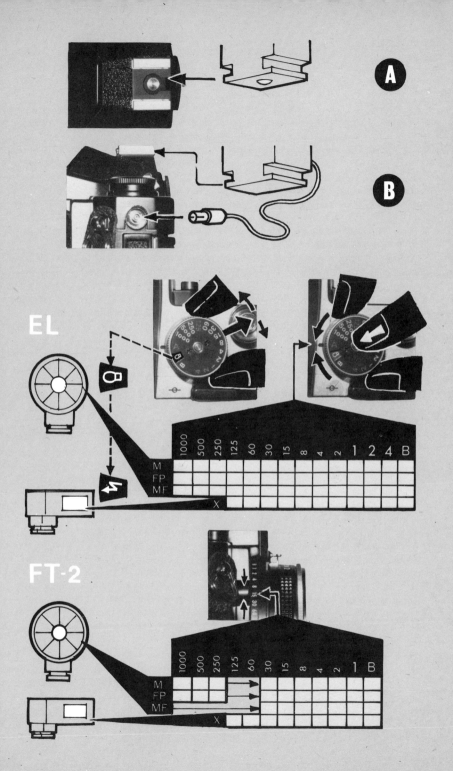

A

B

EL

	1000	500	250	125	60	30	15	8	4	2	1	2	4	B
M														
FP														
MF														
X														

FT-2

	1000	500	250	125	60	30	15	8	4	2	1	B
M												
FP												
MF												
X												

Checking and changing batteries

The exposure metering systems of the cameras, and the shutter speed control of the EL (on auto or manual operation) use batteries. In normal life these batteries last for six months to a year or more, but they should be checked immediately after fitting, at regular intervals, and when the camera has been stored for any length of time. When fitting new batteries, handle them as little as possible and by the edges only. Before putting them in the camera, give them a good rub with a rough dry cloth.

EL

The meter, automatic control, and shutter timing mechanism are powered by a 6 volt silver oxide cell (a manganese alkaline one may be used, but will have a shorter life) housed in the bottom of the mirror box. When the battery is exhausted, the meter may work erratically and the shutter timing correspond neither to the meter indication on Automatic, nor to the speed set manually on the dial. If the battery is completely flat, or has been removed, however, the meter needle will remain static in the centre of the scale, and the shutter will operate at 1/90 sec wherever the dial is set.

The battery is checked with the button on the back of the top-plate. Use a finger-nail or nail-file to press it firmly in. If the light beside it glows a bright orange, then the battery is good. If it does not, replace the battery immediately. If you do not have a spare battery, the safest policy is to remove the existing one, and remember that the shutter will be set to 1/90 sec.

To replace a battery, remove the lens, lock up the mirror with the lock-up lever on the right of the lens-mount, and push the battery compartment lid to the left. Let the existing battery slide out, and put in a new one. Make sure that the positive terminal is to the right (as you look at the mirror box). Snap down the lid, lower the mirror and replace the lens. Take special care during the whole operation not to damage or dirty the inside of the mirror box.

FT2

The FT2 meter is powered by a 1.5 volt silver oxide cell (Mallory MS76 or equivalent) housed in the base plate. When the battery is exhausted, the meter will stop working immediately. It is unlikely that a nearly flat battery will give spurious exposure readings. Once the meter ceases to function, the battery must be replaced before the exposure meter can be used. The camera's normal picture-taking functions, however, in no way depend on the battery.

When it is necessary to fit a new battery, turn the battery cover a quarter turn clockwise with a small coin. Put the new battery in with the positive (+) side showing uppermost. Replace the cover in its bayonet mount, and give it a quarter turn counter-clockwise. This operation needs some care if you are to avoid scuffing the coin slot.

TOP Nikkormat EL

A Checking battery.
B Changing battery.
1 Raise mirror.
2 Open battery cover.
3 Replace battery and close cover.

BOTTOM Nikkormat FT2

Bayonet mount lens cover is removed with a coin. Battery goes in with positive (plus) terminal showing.

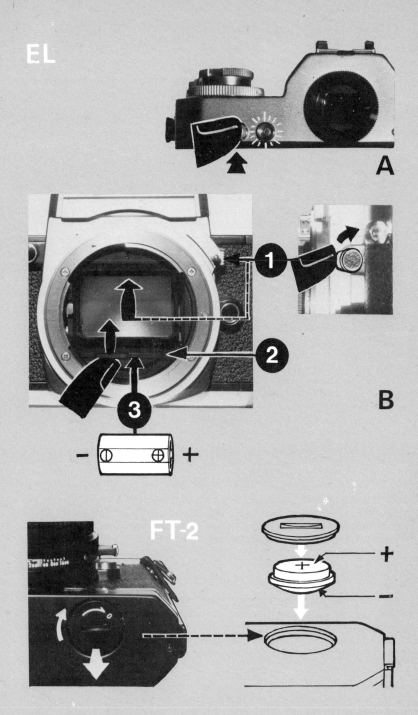

EL

A

B

1

2

3

− +

FT-2

+

−

Interchangeable lenses

When shooting with automatic lenses, including the standard lenses, the diaphragm closes down to the preselected aperture immediately before the shutter opens, and opens up immediately afterwards. All Nikkor 'Auto' lenses have this facility.

All the current range of automatic Nikkor lenses have meter coupling prongs, with the exception of the 200 mm f5.6 Medical-Nikkor, and the long focus lenses used with the Focusing Unit. Without the prong, you must meter in the stop-down mode. With it coupled to the meter you must use the full-aperture method.

Certain specialised lenses, including the PC (Perspective Control), Reflex (Mirror) Nikkors and 1200 mm f11 Nikkor P lenses have their aperture selected manually. In the case of the mirror lenses, there is no diaphragm, and brightness is altered with neutral density filters. Other manual lenses must be stopped down for metering, and for exposure. All automatic Nikkor lenses operate manually unless they are mounted on the camera or on an 'automatic' accessory. A number of older lenses, and the current PC lenses have a preset mechanism comprised of two aperture setting rings. When metering, the required aperture is set on the front ring, which has stiff click-stops and must be pulled back slightly to move: the diaphragm can then be opened with the back ring, which moves easily and operates the iris. Immediately before picture-taking, this ring is used to stop down the diaphragm to the preselected point.

Lens changing

To remove a lens from a Nikkormat camera set the diaphragm to f5.6 if it is meter coupled, press in the lens release button (to the right of the lens), and turn the lens to the right (clockwise) until it can be lifted out. To fit another lens; set its aperture ring to f5.6 (meter coupled lenses); line up the meter coupling prong on the lens with the meter coupling pin on the camera (non-coupled lenses have a black or white dot which must be aligned with the pin); gently push in the lens and turn it counter-clockwise until it clicks into place. To set the meter to the lens' maximum aperture, turn the aperture ring round to its minimum setting (largest f number), and then back to its maximum aperture. The setting can be checked by the position of the red mark below the scale (1.2–2.8–5.6) by the lens release button on the FT2, and on the opposite side on the EL. When using non-coupled lenses, make sure that the meter coupling pin is as far to the right (as you look at the lens mount) as it will go.

Lens designations

Each lens is marked with its maximum aperture and focal length; thus Nikkor 1:1.8 f = 85 mm is an 85 mm lens with a maximum aperture of f1.8.

Many independent manufacturers also supply lenses to fit Nikkormat cameras, some of which are of excellent quality. If you have the slightest difficulty in fitting any lens to your camera, return it to your dealer for modification. *Do not use force.*

A Removing a lens
1 Set to f5.6
2 Press release button
3 Turn clockwise
4 Lift off lens

B Replacing a lens
1 Set meter pin to right.
2 Set lens to f5.6.
3 Line up prong with pin, push in lens and turn.
4 Turn to min, then max aperture, to set meter.

C Features of Nikkor Auto lenses
1 Aperture ring.
2 Focus ring.
3 Focus scale.
4 Depth-of-field scale.
5 Aperture, focus index.
6 Meter coupling prong.
7 Cut-out for lens catch.
8 Bayonet mount.
9 Diaphragm.

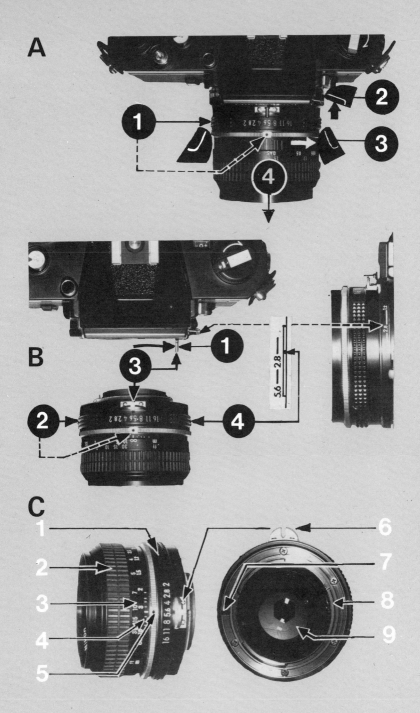

Fisheye lenses

The Nikkor range of fisheye lenses includes two 6 mm, an 8 mm, a 10 mm and a 16 mm lens, each designed for a specific purpose. Because their bulging elements make front fitments impossible, the lenses each have a range of built-in filters. These lenses were originally designed for scientific and surveillance applications, but are now used to give creative flexibility in a wide range of situations. Their striking effects, however, should be used with care to avoid monotony. Apart from the circular image and barrel distortion, these lenses have an enormous depth of field at quite large apertures.

The 6 mm f2.8 and 6 mm f5.6 Fisheye Nikkors both have a picture angle of 220° and produce the now well-known circular image (using equidistant projection). The 6 mm f2.8 lens is nearly 240 mm (9$\frac{3}{8}$ in) in diameter, can be stopped down to f22, and features an automatic diaphragm with coupling prong for full aperture metering. The 6 mm f5.6 lens is much smaller (92 mm, 3$\frac{5}{8}$ in) and lighter, but has a manual diaphragm and no coupling prong. Also its construction does not allow room for the mirror to move between its rear element and the film. Thus the mirror must be locked up, and the lens used with the accessory Fisheye finder, which can be mounted on the accessory shoe. This does not give quite a full view, as the lens itself gets in the way.

The 8 mm f2.8 Fisheye Nikkor and 10 mm f5.6 OP Fisheye Nikkor lenses both give a 180° circular image, but use differently calculated projection systems. The 8 mm f2.8 lens is of the normal equidistant type in which the reproduction size of any part of the subject is determined by its angle from the centre of the lens. The lens has a full aperture prong, and an automatic diaphragm, making it probably the most useful of the circular fisheyes for creative use. The 10 mm OP lens, on the other hand, has an orthographic type of projection, in which the relative size of reproduction is determined by the size of its zenith angle. This results in a considerable proportional increase in the size of parts of the subject recorded in the centre of the image. The image is slightly smaller than that produced by the 8 mm f2.8 lens.

The 16 mm f3.5 Fisheye Nikkor produces a full-frame image with a diagonal angle of about 170°. This lens also exhibits the characteristic barrel distortion, although it is not quite so marked. It is intended for general effects photography, but if the short focal length is all you require, you may find that the 15 mm f5.6 wide angle (see p. 60) lens is as spectacular, and it is a more useful general purpose lens.

TOP
The f2.8 6 mm Fisheye Nikkor and a typical picture.

Fisheye Nikkor Lens Data

Focal length	Angle	Aperture Min	Max	Min. focus m	ft	Diameter mm	in	Length mm	in	Weight g	oz
6 mm	220°	2.8	22	0.3	1	235	9$\frac{3}{8}$	170	6$\frac{1}{4}$	5200	185
6 mm	220°	5.6	22	fixed		90	3$\frac{5}{8}$	80	3$\frac{1}{4}$	430	15
8 mm	180°	2.8	22	0.3	1	125	4$\frac{7}{8}$	140	5$\frac{1}{2}$	1000	35
10 mm	180°	5.6	22	fixed		85	3$\frac{1}{4}$	105	4$\frac{1}{8}$	400	14
16 mm	170°	3.5	22	0.3	1	68	2$\frac{1}{4}$	60	2$\frac{3}{8}$	330	12

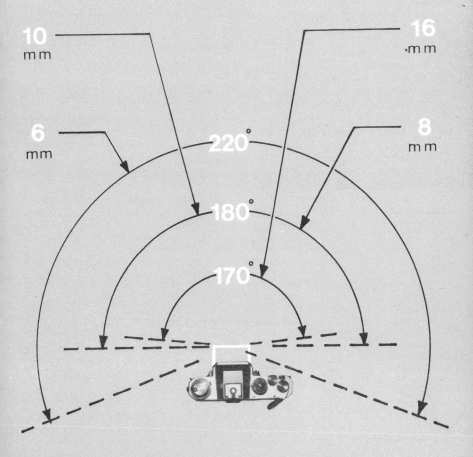

10 mm

16 mm

6 mm

8 mm

220°

180°

170°

Wide angle lenses

The Nikkor range of wide angle lenses includes three 35 mm lenses and three 28 mm lenses offering choices of maximum aperture, a 24 mm, two 20 mm an 18 mm and a 15 mm lens. They are all of 'reversed telephoto' construction, allowing them to be mounted far enough from the film plane to leave room for the mirror to move up and down. This was not the case with some older very wide-angle lenses, which, although somewhat retrofocus, had to be used with the mirror locked up and an accessory viewfinder.

The 35 mm lenses are often classed as 'wide standard' lenses, and are useful for taking in more of the subject than a 50 mm lens, and giving greater depth of field at any particular aperture. Used for general purpose photography, they yield acceptable perspective, but can give 'wide-angle distortion' if required. The choice of maximum aperture depends on the use to which the lens is to be put. For most purposes the f2.8 lens is perfectly adequate; but if you habitually take photographs under low light conditions, the extra bulk and cost of the f2 or f1.4 lens may be justified.

The 28 mm lenses are regarded by many photographers as the upper limit of true wide angles, and this focal length is increasingly being chosen as the first accessory lens. These lenses can be used to give a broad view, although distant objects may in some cases appear so small as to be insignificant. They are also extremely useful when shooting in confined spaces, but in such conditions need care to produce natural looking pictures. The choice between the f2, f2.8 and f3.5 lenses depends largely on the use to which the lens will be put.

The extremely wide angle 24 mm f2.8 and 20 mm f3.5 and f4 Nikkors are more likely to be used for special effects than just to include as much of a view as possible. Because of their extensive depth of field even at quite large apertures, they can be used to picture small close-by objects sharply and larger than life against a much reduced but still sharp background. Another use is in obtaining pictures of high buildings without the converging verticals which appear if you tilt the camera even slightly upwards to take in the top. Naturally, you get an immense amount of foreground as well, but this can be cropped out later. As with all wide-angle lenses, however, care must be taken to keep the camera back exactly vertical, otherwise any convergence will be emphasised by the large field of these lenses.

The 18 mm f4 and 15 mm f5.6 lenses are the widest available. Their use is similar to the 24 and 20 mm lenses, but they have an even wider angle of view and greater depth of field.

Wide angle Nikkor Lenses

Focal Length	Angle	Aperture Min	Max	Min. focus m	ft	Diameter mm	in	Length mm	in	Weight g	oz
15mm	110°	5.6	22	0.3	1	92	$3\frac{5}{8}$	88.5	$3\frac{1}{2}$	700	24.7
18mm	100°	4	22	0.3	1	89	$3\frac{1}{2}$	58.5	$2\frac{1}{4}$	315	11
20mm	94°	3.5	22	0.3	1	75	3	69.5	$2\frac{3}{4}$	390	13.8
20mm	94°	4	22	0.3	1	63.5	$2\frac{1}{2}$	47.5	$1\frac{7}{8}$	210	7.5
24mm	84°	2.8	16	0.3	1	64.5	$2\frac{1}{2}$	59.5	$2\frac{3}{8}$	290	10.2
28mm	74°	2	22	0.3	1	64.5	$2\frac{1}{2}$	70	$2\frac{3}{4}$	345	12.2
28mm	74°	3.5	16	0.6	2	62.5	$2\frac{1}{2}$	54	$2\frac{1}{8}$	215	7.6
28mm	74°	2.8	22	0.3	1	63.5	$2\frac{1}{2}$	54	$2\frac{1}{8}$	240	8
35mm	62°	2	16	0.3	1	63.5	$2\frac{1}{2}$	61	$2\frac{3}{8}$	285	10.1
35mm	62°	1.4	22	0.3	1	66.5	$2\frac{5}{8}$	74.5	$2\frac{7}{8}$	415	14.6
35mm	62°	2.8	22	0.3	1	63.5	$2\frac{1}{2}$	54	$2\frac{1}{8}$	240	8

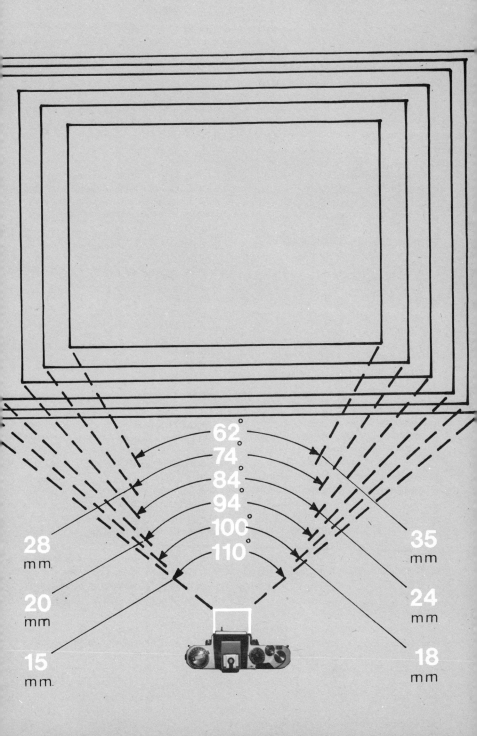

62
74
84
94
100
110

28 mm

35 mm

20 mm

24 mm

15 mm

18 mm

PC and GN Nikkors

PC Lenses

The 28 mm *f*4 and 35 mm *f*2.8 PC Nikkors are lenses which are mounted so that they can be shifted laterally on their barrels. Their most obvious use is to take pictures of buildings without tilting the camera, so that the sides come on parallel and vertical. This is especially useful when taking horizontal format shots of two or three storey buildings, but most dramatic for vertical pictures of higher structures. You can also (by shifting the lens sideways) take a square-on picture of a subject when you can't get directly in front of it. If the camera is firmly mounted on a tripod a sideways shift (from maximum one way to maximum the other) can also be used to take two pictures for a panoramic view.

Mount the lens in the normal way. Decide which way you want to shift it, and rotate it so that the thumbscrew (11) is on the opposite side. Look through the viewfinder and twist the screw until the picture is right. The distance shifted (in mm) is shown by the dot (10) on the scale (9). The figure (1) against the white dot (2) shows how far you can shift the lens without risking deterioration or vignetting in the corners.

The diaphragms are of the preset type. Press in the front ring (13) and turn it until the required aperture setting (14) is against the dot (12). The ring clicks into place. For metering or exposing, the lens is stopped down by moving the inner ring (5) so that its dot (6) aligns with the other. Both rings must move together (with their dots aligned) for metering, which is in the stop-down mode (see p. 36).

(When closing down the lens, the image in the viewfinder may darken unevenly if the lens is shifted far from centre. This does not influence the picture as long as the specified limits are observed.)

The lenses have normal focus rings (4) and scales (8), depth-of-field indicators (7) and IR marks (3).

GN Lens

The 45 mm *f*2.8 GN Auto Nikkor is a small, light lens on which the focusing and aperture rings may be interlocked for photography with a flash unit on the camera. The focus ring is turned until the prong (5) is opposite the guide number for the flash unit. The yellow scale (6) is in feet, and the white one in meters. The prong is then pushed across to surround the appropriate number, locking the two rings together. If your flash guide number (see p. 115) is not on the lens, use the nearest lower number.

Once set, the lens automatically gives the correct aperture for a flash gun on the camera, as it is focused on the subject.

In all other respects, it is a normal automatic-diaphragm lens with focus scale (1) and index (2), aperture scale (3) and meter coupling prong (4). It is a good choice as a standard lens, because it is exceptionally small and light, and could be convenient even if you never use the guide number function. Its small minimum aperture of *f*32 may be particularly useful in some circumstances.

A. PC-Nikkor 35 mm *f*2.8
TOP
Lens in normal position needs camera tilt to take in subject.
CENTRE
With lens shifted upward, there is no need to tilt

B. GN-Auto Nikkor 45 mm *f*2.8
The aperture and focus rings can be interlocked to suit your guide numbers. For keys, see text above.

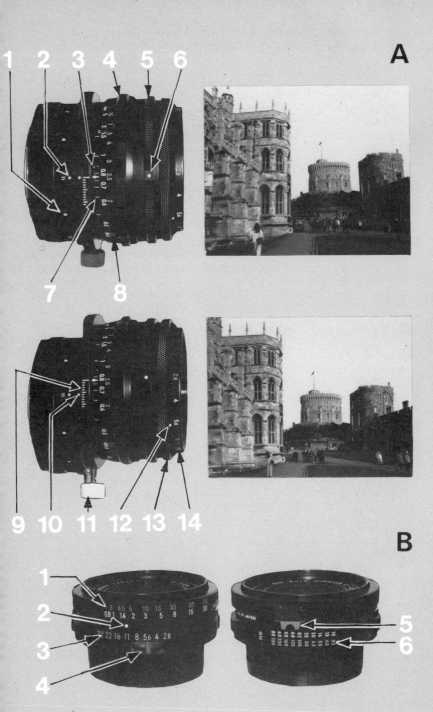

Standard and short tele lenses

The choice of a normal lens for general purpose photography is a subject of great contention. Many photographers like to use a 35 mm lens as standard. They prefer it to a 50 mm lens for the wider view and the greater depth of field at moderate apertures. Other photographers, however, prefer to regard lenses in the 75–90 mm range as their standard; so the almost universal choice of standard lens between 50 and 60 mm for SLR cameras is a good compromise. Nikon produce three such lenses for their cameras. The 55 mm f1.2 Nikkor has the widest aperture, so producing the brightest viewfinder image and the easiest focusing. Its extra light-passing ability is useful under conditions of extremely low light, although the 50 mm f1.4 Nikkor is a more popular wide aperture lens. The 50 mm f2 lens is quite fast enough for the majority of photographers and is probably the most commonly used Nikkor lens.

All the lenses will prove highly satisfactory in a wide range of picture taking situations. An alternative to them is provided by the incredibly small and light 45 mm f2.8 GN Nikkor (see p. 62) which allows automatic flash aperture control; or the 55 mm f3.5 Micro Nikkor (see p. 74); by sacrificing two or three stops in speed, which many photographers seldom use, this lens gives you a considerable gain in close-up ability, especially if you intend to use attachments such as a slide copier.

Some photographers forego a 50–60 mm lens, preferring to use a 35 mm and an 85 mm alternately. Others find that they use moderately long focus lenses almost exclusively. That is, lenses in the 85 to 105 mm range.

Medium telephotos

The 85 mm f1.8 Nikkor has a conveniently large maximum aperture for shooting indoors; and this focal length is much favoured by professional photographers for portraits, as it produces a pleasing perspective in head-and-shoulders pictures. It is particularly suitable as a 'normal' lens for those who find the 50–60 mm lenses include too much unwanted surroundings in their pictures.

For those who want a slightly longer lens there is the 105 mm f2.5 Nikkor. It is quite good for portraits and also for some outdoor work. It gives twice the image size of a standard lens, and is a better complement for this than an 85 mm lens.

Normal and Medium Focus Nikkor Lenses

Focal Length	Angle	Aperture		Min. focus		Diameter		Length		Weight	
		Min	Max	m	ft	mm	in	mm	in	g	oz
50mm	46°	2	16	0.6	2	64.5	$2\frac{1}{2}$	48	$1\frac{7}{8}$	205	7.2
50mm	40°	1.4	16	0.6	2	67	$2\frac{5}{8}$	56.5	$2\frac{1}{4}$	325	11.5
55mm	43°	1.2	16	0.6	2	73.5	$2\frac{7}{8}$	58.3	$2\frac{1}{4}$	420	14.8
85mm	28°30′	1.8	22	1.0	3.5	72	$2\frac{3}{4}$	70	$2\frac{3}{4}$	420	14.8
105mm	23°20′	2.5	32	1.0	3.5	66	$2\frac{5}{8}$	78	3	435	15.3

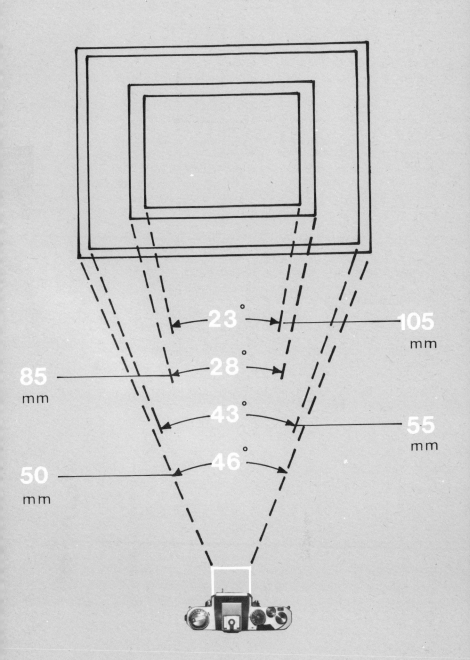

Moderately long focus lenses

Although lenses in the 85 to 105 mm range are widely used for portrait work, and have considerable value out of doors, there are many occasions when greater magnification is useful. A tele-extender (see p. 72) can be used to extend the range of other lenses, but for regular use a longer focus lens is usually the best answer.

The choice of long focus lens or lenses depends largely on personal preference, but lenses between 135 and 400 mm allow a degree of perspective control and subject isolation. They can be hand-held with some care, and do not introduce the problems associated with really long focus lenses. The 135 mm lenses are popular with outdoor photographers. They are long enough for most distant views, and yet can still just be used for occasional portraits. They are probably the best choice as a first telephoto when building up an outfit. The two Auto Nikkors differ in maximum aperture. Although the wider (f2.8) aperture may sometimes prove useful, for many uses the advantages of the lighter and cheaper f3.5 lens can outweigh this.

Often a somewhat greater image magnification is needed. For sports photography and mobile nature work, a hand-held lens is essential. The 200 mm f4 Nikkor Auto offers reasonable magnification, while still being a conveniently hand-held lens. It would be a particularly useful addition for the photographer who already own an 85 or 105 mm lens. The 180 mm f2.8 offers a wider aperture with a slightly smaller image, but is heavier. However, probably the most versatile long telephoto lens is a 300 mm, which has a high enough magnification for most sport and bird photography; the 300 mm f4.5 Nikkor is reasonably dimensioned for hand holding and is fitted with a bush for tripod mounting when possible. The 400 mm f5.6 Nikkor Auto is the longest focal length normal Nikon lens. It is rather large and heavy, best used on a tripod. It should be considered as a complement to a 180 or 200 mm lens.

As well as magnifying the image, a long focus lens also magnifies any movement, in the subject or in the camera. To arrest subject movement you need high shutter speeds, even at the expense of depth of field, and camera shake can be avoided only with a really steady hold. If 1/30 sec just gives a sharp image with a 50 mm lens, 1/125 is needed with a 200 mm if the camera can be held as steady. When using a lens of 200 mm or more, you should always support the lens barrel with your left hand and, if possible, brace yourself or the camera against a firm object. Under most circumstances, these lenses reveal their true optical quality only if used on a tripod or other firm mounting.

Long Focus Nikkor Lenses

Focal Length	Angle	Aperture Min	Max	Min. focus m	ft	Diameter mm	in	Length mm	in	Weight g	oz
135mm	18°	2.8	22	1.5	5	72.5	$2\frac{7}{8}$	104	$4\frac{1}{8}$	620	21.9
135mm	18°	3.5	32	1.5	5	66	$2\frac{1}{2}$	93.5	$3\frac{3}{4}$	460	16.2
180mm	13°	2.8	32	1.8	6	81	$3\frac{1}{4}$	141	$5\frac{5}{8}$	830	29.3
200mm	12°	4	32	2.0	7	72.5	$2\frac{7}{8}$	163	$6\frac{1}{2}$	630	22.2
										kg	lbs
300mm	8°	4.5	22	4.0	13	80	$3\frac{1}{4}$	203	8	1.1	2.3
400mm	6°	5.6	32	5.0	16	85	$3\frac{3}{8}$	262	$10\frac{3}{8}$	1.4	3.1

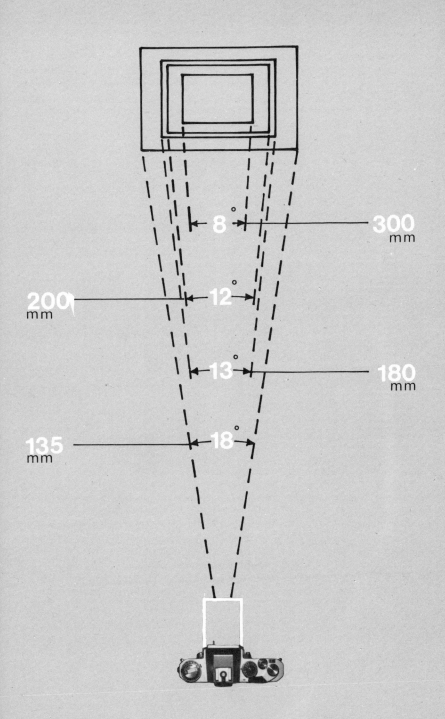

Extreme long focus lenses

Lenses used with the focusing unit

Four very long focus lens heads (400 mm f4.5, 600 mm f5.6, 800 mm f8 and 1200 mm f11) are used with the Nikon Focusing Unit. The focusing unit provides for the normal focusing movement, and includes an automatic-diaphragm mechanism. Because the focusing movement is the same for each lens, the minimum focus distance increases with focal length; thus with the 400 mm f4.5 you can focus down to 5 m (16 ft) whereas with the 1200 mm f11 unit, only to 43 m (140 ft). The lens heads are fitted with their own manually set diaphragm, and this must be set to maximum aperture if the automatic diaphragm is to be used. Of course, setting a larger figure on the automatic diaphragm does *not* increase the maximum aperture of the head. Thus, f8 is the largest usable aperture with the 800 mm f8 head. The focusing unit diaphragm must be set to f4.5 if the lens diaphragm is used. This is essential with the 1200 mm f11 head, as use of the automatic system may result in vignetting.

Reflex Nikkor Mirror lenses

Nikon make mirror lenses in three focal lengths: 500 mm f8, 1000 mm f11 and 2000 mm f11. They all use a combination of mirror surfaces and normal glass refracting elements, enabling the light paths to be folded to produce much shorter and somewhat lighter lenses. They are, however, fatter than comparable all-refracting units. The 500 mm f8 lens is in fact lighter and shorter than the 400 mm f5.6 all-glass lens (p. 66), although it is somewhat larger in diameter. It should be considered seriously as an alternative to the refracting lens. Because the light enters a mirror lens through an annular opening, it is not possible to fit the lenses with conventional diaphragms. The effect of stopping down is obtained by placing a neutral density filter in a slot at the rear of the lens. This affects the light transmission, but not the depth of field, which is determined only by the maximum aperture. Some photographers stop down by fitting an opaque cover which restricts light entry to one quarter of the front area of the lens. This gives some increase in depth of field, and removes the characteristic annular highlights that mirror lenses produce in out-of-focus areas.

Using extremely long lenses

These 'super-telephotos' are really for specialist use only. However, the 500 mm Reflex Nikkor is light enough to be hand held—albeit with some difficulty—and may be used like a moderately long focus lens. Despite this, none of these lenses show their true optical qualities unless they are firmly mounted. They are fitted with tripod bushes which should be used for mounting. Apart from the problem that the minutest camera movement will result in a blurred image, when photographing extremely distant subjects you are shooting through a great depth of atmosphere. Use stop-down metering.

Extreme Long Focus Nikkor Lenses

Focal Length mm	Angle	Aperture Min	Max	Min. focus m	ft	Diameter mm	in	Length mm	in	Weight kg	lbs
400	6°10'	4.5	22	0.5	16	135	5⅜	471.5	18½	3.1	6.8
600	4°10'	5.6	22	11	35	135	5⅜	516.5	20⅜	3.6	7.9
800	3°	8	22	19	61	135	5⅜	711.5	28	3.5	7.7
1200	2°	11	64	43	139	135	5⅜	922	36⅜	4.3	9.5
500	5°		8	0.4	13	93	3⅝	141.5	5½	1	2.2
1000	2°30'		11	0.8	25	117	4⅝	238	9⅜	1.9	4.2
2000	1°10'		11	20	60	262	10⅜	598	23½	17.5	38.6

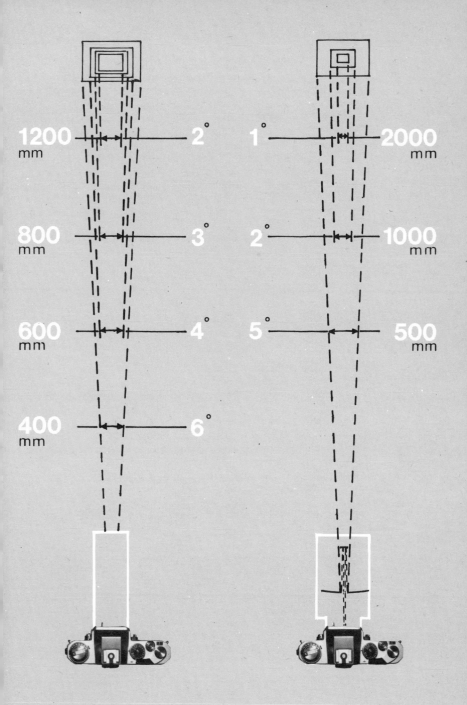

1200 mm   2°

1°   2000 mm

800 mm   3°

2°   1000 mm

600 mm   4°

5°   500 mm

400 mm   6°

Zoom lenses

Zoom lenses are constructed so that you can alter their focal length while the image remains in focus and the f-number remains the same. This allows you to frame the picture exactly as you want—within the limits of the lens. A zoom lens is a useful accessory, which can take the place of two or more different fixed focal length lenses, but has the disadvantage that its physical characteristics are determined by its longest focal length. Thus the 80–200 mm Zoom Nikkor has a maximum aperture of f4.5 and weighs 830 g (29 oz). Although these figures are quite acceptable for a 200 mm lens, they compare unfavourably with data for the 85 mm f1.8 Nikkor lens and the zoom would make a poor substitute for this lens alone. When used over its whole range, however, its versatility is unrivalled, particularly for taking transparencies, because their final composition must be decided in the camera viewfinder. A hand-holdable zoom such as this is also useful for taking negatives in a fixed situation such as a wedding or at the zoo, when its whole range is likely to be used. The shorter zoom lenses are much less of a burden if carried on the camera in place of the standard lens than they are if carried separately.

The Zoom Nikkor 28–45 mm f4.5 covers the range of most commonly used wide angle lenses, and makes a good substitute for a 50 mm standard lens, especially if you often use your camera in confined spaces. The 50–300 mm f4.5 lens makes a rather bulky companion to this, but does replace the standard lens and all the commonly used long focus lenses. Both these zoom lenses have separate zooming and focusing rings.

Like the remaining Zoom Nikkors, the 80–200 mm f4.5 lens is focused by rotating its black rubberised grip, and zoomed by moving the same grip back and forward. It requires an exceptionally steady hand to maintain exact focus throughout the zoom, and you would be well advised to refocus after reframing the picture. Like the 28–45 mm and 50–300 mm lenses, the 80–200 mm Zoom Nikkor has an automatic diaphragm, and a meter coupling prong for full aperture metering.

The 180–600 mm f8 and 200–600 mm f9.5 Zoom Nikkors give great versatility to the super telephoto user. They have automatic diaphragms but must be metered in the stop-down mode. They are, however, large and relatively heavy pieces of equipment, intended to be used on a tripod, for which they are fitted with bushes.

The largest and most impressive Zoom Nikkor is the 360–1200 mm f11 lens. It focuses down to 6 m (20 ft), which is extremely close for a 'super-telephoto' length lens. Because of its bulk and weight, its use must be confined to places where a firm static mounting can be used.

Zoom Nikkor Lenses

Focal Length mm	Angle	Aperture Min	Max	Min. focus m	ft	Diameter mm	in	Length mm	in	Weight kg	lbs
28–45	74°–50°	4.5	22	0.6	2	75	3	91	$3\frac{1}{8}$	435	15.3
43–86	53°–28°	3.5	22	1.2	4	65	$2\frac{1}{2}$	78.2	$3\frac{1}{16}$	410	14.5
50–300	46°–8°10′	4.5	22	2.5	8.5	98	$3\frac{7}{8}$	292	$11\frac{1}{2}$	2.3kg	5.1lbs
80–200	30°10′–12°20′	4.5	32	1.8	6	74.5	3	162	$6\frac{3}{8}$	830	29.3lbs
180–600	13°40′–4°10′	8	32	2.5	8.5	105	$4\frac{1}{8}$	403	16	3.2kg	7.2lbs
200–600	12°20′–4°10′	9.5	32	0.4	13	89	$3\frac{1}{2}$	382	15	2.3kg	5.1lbs
360–1200	6°50′–2°	11	32	0.6	20	125	$5\frac{1}{8}$	704	$27\frac{1}{2}$	6.6kg	13.8lbs

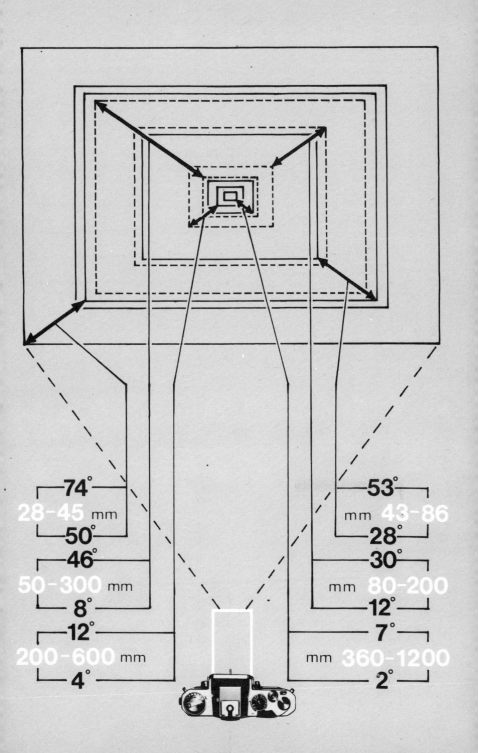

74°
28-45 mm
50°

46°
50-300 mm
8°

12°
200-600 mm
4°

53°
mm 43-86
28°

30°
mm 80-200
12°

7°
mm 360-1200
2°

Tele-extenders

A number of independent lens makers supply tele-extenders which can fit between the lens and the lens mount on Nikkormat cameras. They are sometimes called behind-the-lens converters. They comprise a multi-element negative lens mounted in a short barrel and multiply the focal length of the prime lens by a specific amount. The most common extenders approximately double the focal length. Others treble it and some can be varied between double and treble multiplication.

Exposure

Tele-extenders increase the focal length without altering the effective aperture of the prime lens (see p. 24) so the marked *f*-numbers no longer represent the relative aperture. In fact, they must be multiplied by the power of the extender to give the *f*-number of the combination. Thus a 50 mm *f*1.4 lens becomes a 100 mm *f*2.8 with a 2× extender or a 150 mm *f*4 (4.2) with a 3×. All aperture settings are similarly affected. The Nikkormats' through-the-lens exposure systems take account of this effect and indicate the exposure actually needed. Some tele-extenders are available with automatic diaphragm mechanisms to allow normal diaphragm operation; but some do not couple with the full-aperture metering system and so are used with measurement stop-down. The lens on the EL must be stopped down before the shutter is released when the camera is used for automatic exposure with a non-meter-coupled lens.

Uses

As the photographic effect of the combination is the same as that of a prime lens of equivalent focal length (see p. 124), tele-extenders provide relatively inexpensive means of obtaining telephoto results. They are ideal for taking the occasional photo which needs a longer focal length lens than you normally use and do not add much to the weight and bulk of your equipment. A further bonus is that the combination of lens and extender focuses exactly as does the prime lens, and thus can normally be focused on a subject closer to the camera than could a prime lens of the same effective focal length.

It is possible to use two or more extenders in combination; their effects on focal length and aperture are then multiplied. For example, a 2× and a 3× extender together would turn a 55 mm *f*1.2 into a 330 mm unit with a maximum aperture of *f*8 (7.2).

The use of extenders is not, of course, confined to extending standard lenses. They have an equivalent effect on long focus lenses (a 2× converter makes an *f*2.8 135 mm lens into an *f*5.6 270 mm combination); and even, if needed, on wide-angle lenses.

Disadvantages

Tele-extenders multiply the effects of the prime lens, including any aberrations or other faults. Also, many extenders are of poorer quality than Nikkor prime lenses. As a result, extender/lens combinations do not usually produce pictures quite as sharp as those taken with a prime lens. The conditions that apply to really long focus lenses (see p. 68) also apply to combinations with equivalent focal length. In many circumstances, too, the small relative aperture of the combination can be a disadvantage. The intention to use an extender is a good reason for choosing wide aperture prime lenses.

Tele-extenders

Placed behind the lens, a tele-extender multiplies the focal length.
1 Normal 50 mm lens picture.
2 Picture with 2× converter behind lens.

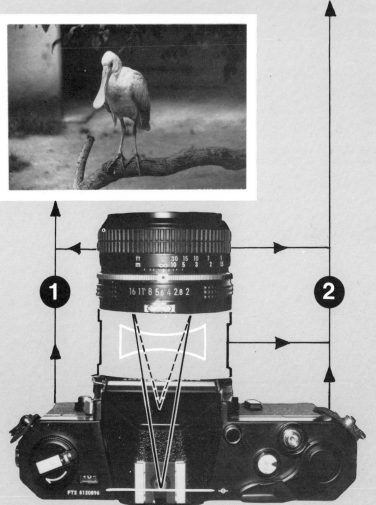

Macro and Bellows lenses

The standard Nikkor lens will focus to about 50 mm (24 in) from the film plane (indicated by the -o- mark). To focus more closely with the normal lens, thus producing a larger image on the film, either the lens must be moved further from the camera—using extension tubes (see p. 78) or bellows (see p. 80)—or it must be fitted with an auxiliary lens (see p. 12).

Micro-Nikkor lenses

Micro-Nikkor lenses are designed to focus closer than normal lenses of equivalent focal length. They are computed to give optimum performance at close range, but also give good results at normal distances. They are coupled for automatic diaphragm and full aperture metering.

The 55 mm f3.5 Micro Nikkor Auto lens can focus from infinity down to about 24 cm ($9\frac{1}{2}$ in) from the film plane. It gives a magnification of $\frac{1}{2}\times$ and also allows greater than normal magnification when used with extension tubes or bellows. It uses accessory extension ring M2 to allow life-size reproductions, but loses its automatic diaphragm facility. The 55 mm Micro-Nikkor lens is useful as a 'standard' lens if you don't need the extra aperture of the normal lenses.

The 105 mm f4 Micro Nikkor Auto lens focuses unaided from infinity down to about 45 cm (18 in) from the film plane, also giving a magnification of $\frac{1}{2}\times$. It is an exceedingly useful lens, suited to portrait and candid photography as well as close-up work. With its accessory extension ring PN1, it can give life-size reproduction. With this ring, it retains its automatic aperture facility, and its meter coupling for full aperture exposure measurement.

105 mm f4 Bellows Nikkor

This is a special short-barrelled lens, which allows focusing from infinity to a magnification of more than life size when mounted on a bellows unit. It is fitted with a manual preset aperture mechanism. It is not meter coupled, and metering must be carried out in the stop-down mode.

Macro and bellows lenses

TOP
The Micro-Nikkor 55 mm f3.5 lens has an automatic diaphragm, and focuses close enough to give $\frac{1}{2}$ life-size reproduction. With the M2 ring, it operates manually, and focuses to give pictures up to life size.

MIDDLE
The Micro-Nikkor 105 mm f4 lens works in the automatic mode with or without the PN-1 extension ring it uses to give life-size reproduction.

BOTTOM
The 105 mm f4 Bellows Nikkor fits on to extension bellows to give focus distances from infinity down to a few inches from the lens.

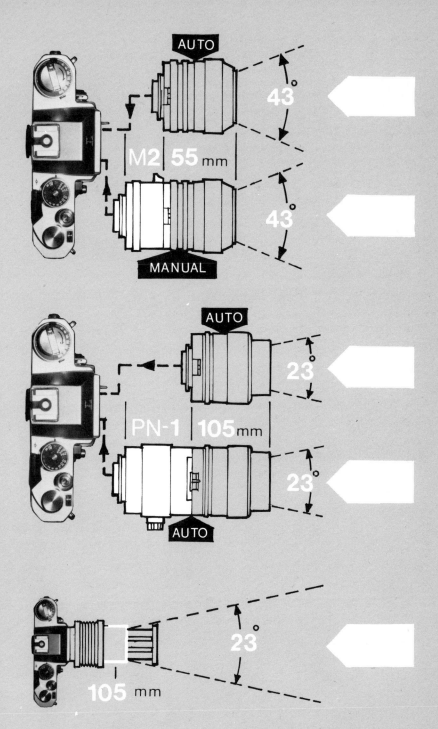

Medical Nikkor lens

The 200 mm *f*5.6 Medical Nikkor is a special close-up lens incorporating a built-in electronic ring-flash unit. It cannot be focused in the normal way, and is supplied with six supplementary lenses (1), giving (singly or in combination) 10 fixed reproduction ratios in addition to the lens' natural focus. The colour-coded diagrams (8) engraved on the lens' front ring indicate the lenses used for the combined ratios. When two supplementaries are combined, always put the most powerful nearest the lens. The lens is fitted to the camera in the usual way, lining up the dot (18) with the meter coupler.

Flash exposure settings
The ASA speed of the film in use is set against the index for full (4) or quarter power (12), as needed, by turning the front ring (5). This is then locked with the milled screw (13). Setting the index at the front of the rear ring to the reproduction ratio on the scale on the front ring (15) sets the aperture for the flash-to-subject distance. This ring can be locked with a milled screw (14). The aperture (*f*-number) in use is indicated by the scale at the back of the ring (16) against the index (17).

The possible range of reproduction ratios is determined by the speed of the film in use. The flash may be set to a quarter of the normal power so that it can be used slightly closer by switching the power pack. If you can't set the rings for a combination of film speed and magnification, you can't use it.

Frame numbering
The milled ring in front of the film speed ring sets the number (from 1 to 39) or the reproduction ratio, which will be printed on the bottom right-hand corner of the frame if so desired. The information to be printed appears in the centre of the cut out (3) against the film speed index. The flash intensity reaching the film is automatically regulated with the aperture setting. The blank space between the two ends of the scale indicates that nothing will be printed on the film.

Power supply and synchronisation
The flash unit needs a separate power source. You can choose between an AC unit or a DC unit (21). Either is fed into the sunken three-pin plug (10) with the connecting cord (20) supplied. A small neon bulb (11) next to the plug indicates when the flash is charged and ready to fire. The charging time between flashes varies from about 6 seconds to about 15 seconds depending on the power source. The flash is fired through its normal 3 mm (PC) socket (2) connected to the camera's flash socket (19) through a cord supplied with the lens. Naturally speeds below 1/125 sec must be used, and the EL must be set to X (⚡).

Pilot lamps
Four 2.5 volt torch bulbs are incorporated as working lights (7). They are switched on by pressing the white button (9) on the right-hand side. If the bulbs fail, they can be replaced after the front (black) cover has been unscrewed and taken off.

Removing the flash unit
Unscrewing the central chrome ring (6) (into which the auxiliary lenses fit) allows the entire unit to be removed from the lens so that it can be used independently.

200 mm *f*5.6 Medical Nikkor lens

For keys see text above.

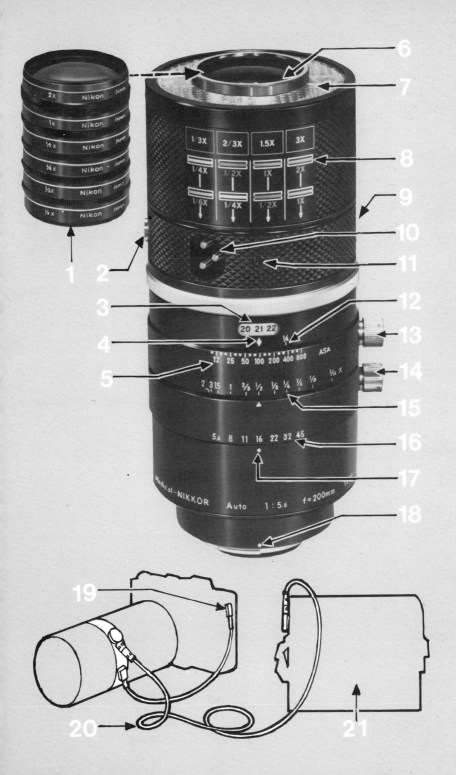

Close-up accessories

Extension tubes

Extension tubes move the lens further from the film plane allowing a closer focusing distance and thus a larger image on the film (see p. 121)

The Nikon Set K rings consist of five tubes in the following lengths: K1, 5.8 mm; K2, 5 mm; K3, 5.8 mm; K4, 10 mm and K5, 20 mm. Ring K1 is fitted to the camera body (aligning the black dot with the meter coupling pin) the lens can then be fitted to this to give a short extension. K2 may be fitted to the body in the same way. K3 is then fitted to the lens. The two rings can be screwed together (giving 10.8 mm—$\frac{2}{5}$ inch—extension); K4, K5 or both can be screwed between them to give the required magnification between 0.11× and life size with a 50 mm standard lens. (The ring K1 may be used as well to give slightly greater extension.) The lens diaphragms operate manually, and metering must be carried out at working aperture.

The Auto Extension Rings consist of three tubes PK-1, 8 mm; PK-2, 14 mm and PK-3, 27.5 mm. They have bayonet mounts each end, and extend the focusing range in the same way as the normal tubes, but allow full aperture metering and automatic diaphragm operation. They may be used singly or in combination.

The extension ring E2 is a single 14 mm tube with a built-in plunger to hold the lens at full aperture directly, or through a Nikon cable release.

Extension tubes can be used with any lens. The shorter the focal length, the greater the magnification at any given extension. Thus, for example, a 28 mm lens gives a magnification of about 2× when used with a full set of extension tubes together, whereas an 85 mm gives about 0.75×.

Reverse adapters

Most normal lenses give better close-up results if they are used back-to-front and should be reversed for magnifications of 1 : 1 or greater. Reversed telephoto lenses (see p. 60) are given extra extension by being reversed. A Macro Adapter Ring BR-2 can be screwed into any 52 mm filter thread to mount the lens backwards on a Nikkormat camera. Used without any other accessory, the adapter acts as a short extension tube, allowing closer than normal focusing.

Adapter Ring BR-3 is a slightly larger adapter used with the PS-4 or PS-5 slide copiers and a reversed lens (see p. 84).

Close-up lenses

Close-up lenses are positive accessory lenses which fit on the front of normal lenses. Their power is measured in dioptres (calculated as one metre divided by their focal length in metres). The greater the power, the closer you can focus and so the greater the magnification. The Nikon close-up lenses screw into 52 mm filter mounts. They are No. 0 (0.5 diopters) No. 1 (1.OD) and No. 2 (2.OD). Lenses No. 1 and 2 in combination give a focused distance of 33 mm (12 in) from the subject. Lens No. 0 is normally used only to reduce the focus distance of telephoto lenses.

A   Extension tubes

1   Set K Rings.
2   Auto Extension Rings set PN.

B   Reverse adapter

C   Close-up lenses

Showing approximate magnifications for No. 0, 1 and 2 lenses.

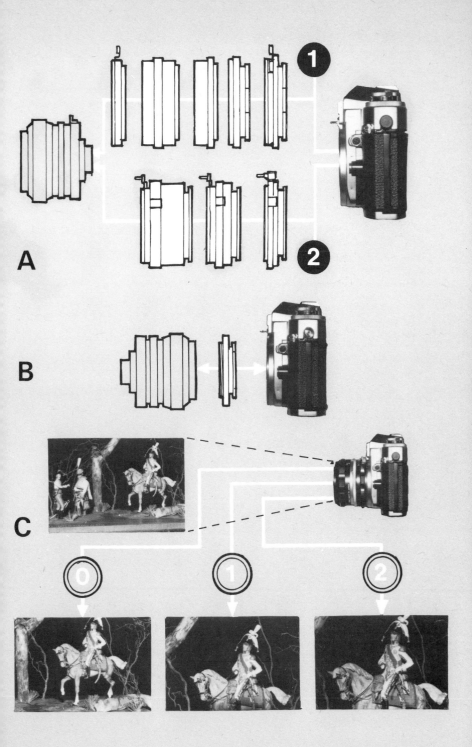

A

B

C

Extension Bellows

Instead of using fixed extension tubes, the lens may be extended on a bellows unit. Bellows comprise two panels mounted on a rail (or on twin rails) and connected by an extensible light proof tube (2). The camera is mounted on one panel, and the lens on the other.

Bellows Focusing Attachment PB-5

The two panels are mounted on twin rails. They are adjusted to the required extension by turning the knobs on the right-hand side (3, 12) (looking from the camera) and may be locked in position by twisting the knobs on the left-hand side (6, 7). When the camera panel (10) is fully back, the lens extension, from 43 to 185 mm is indicated by the position of the front of the lens panel (1) on the scale (11) beside the gear track. If the camera panel is moved, the position of its back edge may be subtracted to give the extension. The unit may be mounted on a support using the bush in the seat (13), or the one in the front support (4).

To mount a camera on the bellows, remove its lens; bayonet this into the lens mount on the front panel (line up the meter coupling prong with the white dot). Then fit the camera body to the rear bayonet mount (9) in the same way. Automatic diaphragm mechanisms act manually, and you must meter in the stop-down mode.

To disassemble the unit, use the lens release button on the camera to release the bellows, and the similar button (14) on the front bellows panel to release the lens.

The hole in the front (between the rails—15) and locking knob (8) is for mounting a slide copier (see p. 84).

Taking photographs

You can use the bellows with the camera panel locked: unlock the lens panel and, using the right-hand knob (7), rack it forward to give the extension you need. Move the whole unit backward and forward to bring your subject into sharp focus. As the depth of field is extremely small, focusing must be very accurate. If the degree of magnification is wrong, move the lens panel to a new setting and refocus. Another method is to lock the lens panel at the front of the rails, set the whole unit at the required lens-to-subject distance, and focus by moving the camera panel back and forward.

However you focus, make sure that both panels are locked and the apparatus firmly supported before you take a picture. Take a stop-down meter reading by adjusting the lens aperture (see p. 36), adjust the camera as necessary and press the shutter release. (Remember that no extra adjustment to the exposure is needed on account of the magnification because the meter reads through the lens.) When the camera is mounted on a support and the shutter speed is slow, there is much less danger of camera shake if you use a cable release (see p. 48).

The bellows may be used with any Nikkor lens, between 24 and 300 mm, but the greatest magnification is obtained with the shortest focal length lenses. The Bellows-Nikkor 105 mm f4 allows focusing from ∞ down to life size reproduction. With normal lenses, the flattest field for magnifications of greater than 1–1 is obtained by using the lens in a reversed position with the Macro Adapter Ring BR-2. The lens may be opened up for focusing conveniently by using the E2 extension ring (see p. 78) and a cable release.

Bellows Focusing Attachment PB5

For keys, see text above.

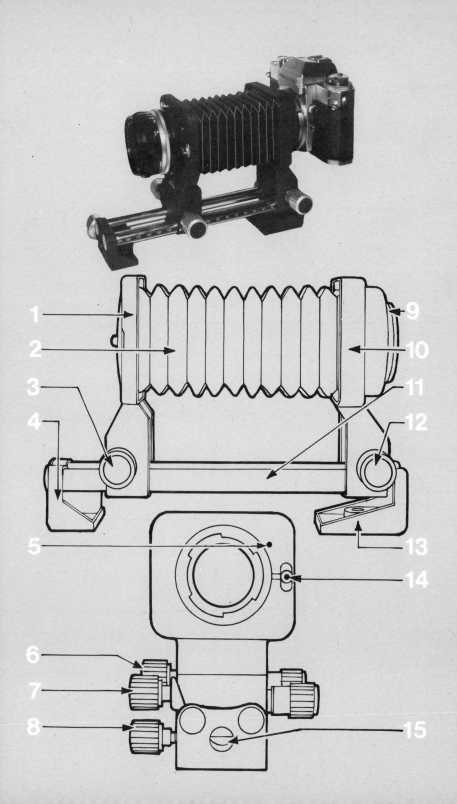

1
2
3
4
5
6
7
8
9
10
11
12
13
14
15

Bellows focusing attachment PB-4

The Bellows PB-4 is a sophisticated four-rail bellows unit of which the front (lens) panel may be tilted or shifted. The base on the lower pair of rails can be racked into any position for focusing, or balancing the unit.

The camera mounting panel is similar to that on the Bellows PB-5, and the camera is mounted on the bayonet in the same way. Either panel is moved by the knobs on the left (looking from the camera) and locked in its desired position by the smaller knobs on the right. The extension from 43 to 180 mm is marked on the upper left-hand rail. As with the PB-5 Bellows, the camera may be set either horizontally or vertically after being released with the button on the lens panel.

The unit is used just like the Bellows PB-5 (see p. 80), with the addition that the attitude and position of the front panel can be altered manually after one of the locking levers has been released. The levers below the lens mount both move to the left to unlock the panel. The upper one allows it to be slid to the left or right. This is useful for exact framing without moving the camera support, and for selecting the area of slide to be copied when using Slide-Copying Adapter PS-5. The lower lever unlocks the swing movement; this movement alters the plane of sharp focus, which sometimes allows more of a subject to be focused sharply. For normal use, the panel is set centrally, with no swing.

The hole in front of the unit is for mounting an accessory slide copier (PS-4 or PS-5). It can be moved in or out on its supporting rod, and clamped in the desired position with the screw on the right-hand side.

Bellows Focusing Attachment PB-4

1	Lens panel	11	Sliding support lock
2	Lens mount	12	Camera panel
3	Shift lock	13	Bellows tube
4	Swing lock	14	Lens line-up dot
5	Lens panel mount	15	Lens release
6	Magnification scale	16	Camera panel movement
7	Slide copier mounting	17	Lens panel movement
8	Horizontal/Vertical camera release	18	Sliding support movement
		19	Tripod bush
9	Camera mount	20	Lens panel lock
10	Panel lock	21	Slide copier lock

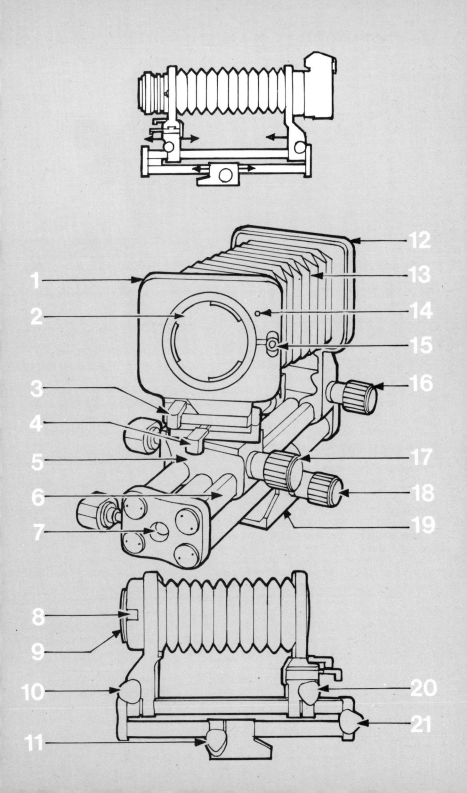

Slide copiers

The Slide Copying Adapters PS-4 and PS-5 are accessories to either of the Bellows Focusing Attachments PB-4 and PB-5. They are affixed by sliding their mounting rod into the hole in the front of the Bellows units. They are clamped in place by the screw on the right of the front mounting of the Attachment. All the normal rules of bellows photography (see p. 80) apply when they are used, except that a tripod is not essential. The whole equipment can simply be stood on a firm support, such as a table.

Slide copying with Adapter PS-5
Use any Nikkor lens between 24 mm and 85 mm (the Micro-Nikkor-P Auto 55 mm f3.5 is particularly suitable for accurate work). Set up the bellows in the normal way. Fit the slide copier to the bellows and tighten the clamping screw.

Set the bellows extension to give the magnification you require (i.e. about 50 mm for 1:1 reproduction with a 50 mm lens). Now pull out the slide copier bellows (it is normally held in place magnetically). Press the button on the top of the plate and fit the retaining ring into the lens filter ring; release the button. When the lens is reversed, use the Adapter Ring BR-3 fitted to the lens bayonet so that the copier bellows can be fitted snugly to the lens. Film strips are held behind a hinged panel with the open glass insert on the front of the copier. Mounted slides are inserted in the slot just behind the film strip slit. Film strips may be moved from side to side within the carrier, but you cannot otherwise choose the exact area you wish to copy.

The image is brought into focus by sliding the slide copier back and forward. If the magnification is suitable, you can now take the picture, but be sure to tighten all locking screws before exposure.

Slide Copying Adapter PS-4
The PS-4 Copier is similar to the PS-5 copier, but has holders to support the coiled ends of long film strips, and the picture area can be trimmed. The slide and film carrier may be moved vertically and horizontally to select the exact picture area to be copied. It is locked in position by the knob on the front. The central position is delineated by click stops. Its use is otherwise identical to that of the PS-5 copier.

Films and exposure
Colour slides and colour negatives may be copied on colour transparency film, and black-and-white transparencies made from negatives on negative film. Colour or black-and-white negatives can be made from slides on the appropriate film; much more sophisticated equipment is needed to make transparencies from colour negatives. The exposure may be made to daylight or an artificial light source, but colour films in the camera must be balanced for it (see p. 107). It is best to reflect the light from an evenly illuminated white card. In a continuous light source, the Nikkormat meters give the correct exposure, but things are less direct with flash. However, a good starting point is to work out the aperture in the usual way using the flash-to-white-card-to-film distance, correct for the magnification (i.e. open up by $1\frac{1}{2}$–2 stops for 1:1) and then open up one more stop. 'Computer' flash units *must* be set to manual if they are to give a known output.

Slide Copying Adapter PS-4

1 Lens flange panel	5 Film strip holder	9 Film strip mount
2 Lens grip button	6 Slide slot	10 Magnetic holder
3 Bellows	7 Movement lock	11 Lens panel grip
4 Attaching rail	8 Opal glass	12 Snap-on lens mount

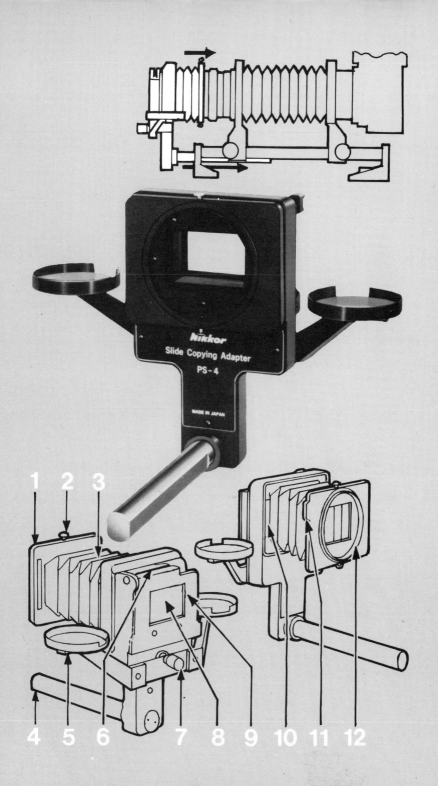

Nikon filters

Filters alter the light (or other radiation) reaching the film (see p.116). Nikon produce a series of filters for use with Nikkor lenses.

For colour transparency films
Coloured filters used with reversal films alter the colour of the final transparency, either for effect or to correct a tendency toward 'incorrect' colour.

Effect of filter on colour slides

Filter	Colour	Effect
Ultra-violet	UV absorbing	Haze cutting. Reduces blue casts.
Skylight	Very pale pink	Similar to UV filter, slightly warmer.
Neutral density	Grey	Reduce light without altering the colour.
Polarizing	Grey	For reducing reflections or darkening skies.
Blue	Light blue	For use with low, red, sunlight.
	Mid blue	For using daylight film with clear flash-bulbs.
	Deep blue	For using daylight film with studio floods.
Amber	Light amber	For daylight film in dull bluish lighting outdoors
	Deep amber	For using type A (tungsten) film in daylight.

For colour negative films
Colour negative films do not need accurate filtration in the camera because the colour balance can be corrected in printing. A polarizing filter acts exactly as it does with transparency films, and UV absorbing filters may afford some degree of haze penetration. Optimum colour can be attained with professional type colour films only if they are approximately balanced to the light source.

For black-and-white films
Polarizing and neutral density filters have the same effect as they do with colour films, and ultra-violet absorbing filters may reduce haze. Coloured filters, however, simply alter the relative tones of different coloured parts of the subject.
 The Nikon range includes two Green, three Yellow, Orange and Red filters.

Availability
All the filters are available in 52 mm mounts; some in other sizes—see opposite.

Gelatin Filters
Filter Holders AF-1 (for 52 mm) and AF-2 (for 72 mm) are used to fit three inch square (e.g. Kodak) gelatin filters to the front of Nikon lenses.

Exposure
Many filters require some increase in exposure. Polarizing filters and colour converting filters have factors (for exposure increase) of several stops, while skylight and UV absorbing filters require no change. The through-the-lens metering of Nikkormat cameras reads through the filter, and indicates an exposure which takes account of the filter factors.

Nikon filters with their common uses.

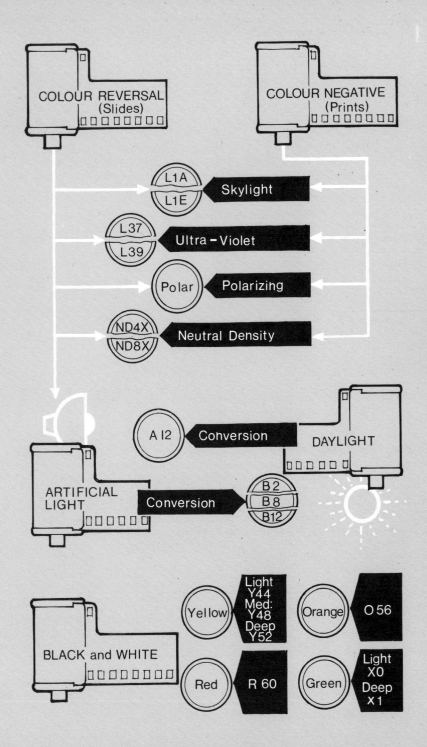

COLOUR REVERSAL
(Slides)

COLOUR NEGATIVE
(Prints)

L1A
L1E
Skylight

L37
L39
Ultra – Violet

Polar
Polarizing

ND4X
ND8X
Neutral Density

A 12
Conversion
DAYLIGHT

ARTIFICIAL
LIGHT
Conversion
B 2
B 8
B12

BLACK and WHITE

Yellow
Light
Y44
Med:
Y48
Deep
Y52

Orange
O 56

Red
R 60

Green
Light
X0
Deep
X1

Tripods and panoramic pictures

Camera supports are necessary to avoid camera shake in pictures taken at shutter speeds longer than 1/30 second (or shorter with long focus lenses), and make photography of static subjects considerably simpler.

Tripods

The most common general purpose support is the tripod. Tripods have three extensible legs which allow them to be stood stably on irregular surfaces and some also have an extensible centre pillar which allows the camera height to be adjusted without disturbing the legs. The tripod head may consist simply of a flat plate with a mounting screw, but many have more complex *pan and tilt* heads. These heads allow the camera to be rotated or tilted independently of tripod movement, and thus simplify lining up the camera with its subject. The camera is fitted to the head by the tripod bush in the case plate. Care must be taken not to over-tighten tripod screws as such action may damage the bush.

Small light-weight tripods are very handy to carry, but do not provide particularly rigid camera supports. For most purposes a sturdy middle weight model will repay its extra bulk. A large heavy tripod may be useful for studio work, but is not easily portable. Whatever type you favour, always spread the legs wide and use the shortest extension compatible with your pictorial aims. This reduces the possibility of camera shake, or of the whole equipment being toppled over.

When setting up the tripod, it is often necessary to ensure that the camera is exactly horizontal. If the tripod is not fitted with a spirit level one may be fitted into the camera's accessory shoe to aid levelling.

A major use of a tripod is in portrait photography. If the camera is firmly supported with all its controls set, the photographer can then concentrate on the subject's poses and expressions. They are also extremely useful in landscape and architectural work. Once the composition has been chosen, the photographer can wait for the moment when the lighting is right, or when people take up just the right positions.

Panoramic views

The widest horizontal angle available with a normal (straight-line) lens is about 100°. To obtain wider views, you must either sacrifice straight-line reproduction or take two or more adjacent pictures. The Panorama Head AP-2 is designed for the latter purpose. It is mounted on a tripod, levelled with its built-in level, and the camera mounted on it. The camera can now be rotated a known amount between exposures to ensure the necessary overlap. The head is rotated the correct amount for 28, 35, 50, 85 or 105 mm lenses in accordance with a calibrated scale. This ensures that the pictures are taken with adequate overlap.

When joining up photographs, cut *half* the overlap off one, then fix it to the adjacent print in exactly the right place. This minimises the effect of size differences which are unavoidably created between the centre and the edge of the image formed by any normal camera lens.

Camera supports

A Table stand/clamp
B Tripod with pan-and-tilt head

C Ball and socket joint
D Panorama Head

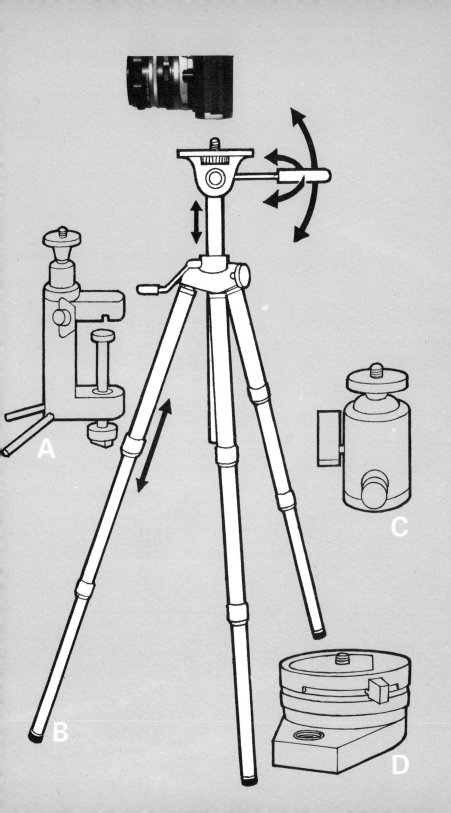

A

B

C

D

Other camera supports

In some situations, you may need to hold the camera especially steady, but be unable to use a conventional tripod (see p. 88), or to carry one with you. There are a number of smaller and more portable devices available.

Hand grips
Two types of hand grips are generally available; pistol grips and side-mounted grips. Both normally include a shutter release, and are connected by a cable to the camera button. Pistol grips are moulded handles which mount immediately below the tripod bush of the camera or lens, and some photographers find them helpful. The Nikon Pistol Grip Model 2 has a large smooth trigger. Side-mounted grips may also be useful. They are mounted on a bar, which bolts along the bottom of the camera like a flash bar. In fact, many of the grips are combined with a flash mounting, and are particularly useful for quick operations at parties and similar functions, as they allow a single flash to be mounted a reasonable distance from the lens.

Shoulder grips
Lightweight supports in the style of rifle stocks are of considerable value when using really long focus lenses. The lens (with the camera attached) is mounted on the support, which has a shoulder pad and a hand-grip with 'trigger'. The whole outfit can be held firmly to the shoulder with the right-hand (or the left-hand for those who view with their left eye) and the lens focused and steadied with the other hand.

Minipods
Lightweight folding table tripods are useful in many circumstances; they can be used to steady the camera against a whole range of supports. Some of them extend to normal tripod height, and although nowhere near stable enough to act as an independent support, they can be used as unipods to aid hand holding.

Document copying
Copying documents is best done with the camera supported at about eye-level to shoot vertically downward. In this position, it is usually much easier to view through the right-angle finder (see p. 50).

The Repro-Copy Outfit, Model PF-2 consists of a base-board with vertical tube clamped to it. An arm bearing a camera support cradle may be clamped at any height with a clamp lever. The cradle is fixed to a focusing rail which is used for fine focusing. The camera can be fitted with whatever close-focusing aids are needed for the reproduction ratio expected (see p. 78). The Repro-Copy Outfit Model PFC-2 is similar to the PF-2, but the base-board is hinged, and folds to form a carrying case. The Model PFT-2 is supplied with a table clamp only (i.e. no base-board).

Illumination for copying should be evenly spread across the subject, and the simplest satisfactory set-up is usually to use two similar lamps, one each side shining from an angle of about 45°. Through-the-lens meter readings are best taken from an 18° grey card on the base-board, and should prove accurate. Otherwise, meter from a white card and give five stops more exposure.

Camera mountings

A Pistol grip.

B Shoulder pod.

C Repro-copy outfit.

D Mini-tripod.

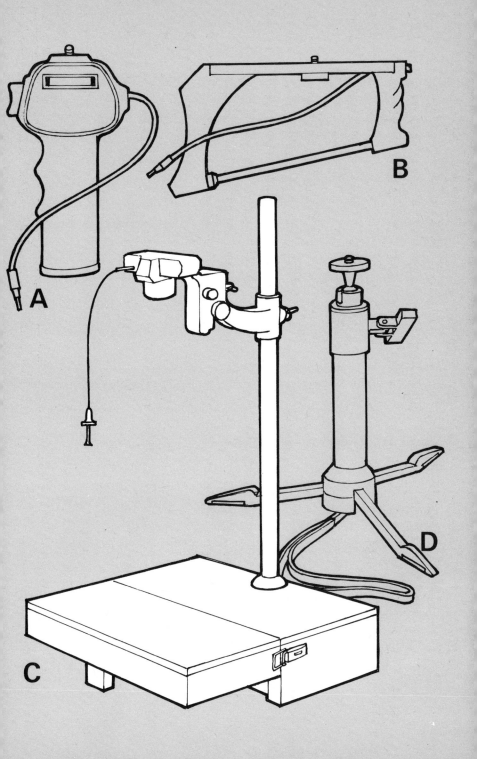

A

B

C

D

Film speeds

Whatever film you use in your camera, it must be given the correct exposure if it is to produce the picture you want. Exposure is the amount of light that falls on the film, and correct exposure is calculated from the light intensity reflected from the subject, and the sensitivity—or speed—of the film in use. Many systems have been used to express film sensitivity, but two are now used widely—ASA (or BS) and DIN.

ASA speeds

The ASA speed is based on testing devised by the American National Standards Institute (formerly the American Standards Association). It is an arithmetical system in which a doubling of the film's sensitivity is denoted by a doubling of the speed rating. Thus in any given condition 100 ASA film requires one stop more (twice) exposure than 200 ASA film, and one stop less (half) than that required by 50 ASA materials.

DIN speeds

The DIN speed ratings are based on German standards, and are expressed on a logarithmic scale. An increase of three points indicates a doubling of the film's sensitivity; thus 50 ASA film is rated at 17 DIN, 100 ASA film at 20 DIN, and 200 ASA film at 23 DIN. The numerical scales cross over at the figure 12, i.e. a 12 ASA film is also rated at 12 DIN.

The scales then go on:

ASA	12	15	20	25	32	50	64	80	100	125	160	200	320	400
DIN	12	13	14	15	16	17	18	19	20	21	22	23	24	25

Film manufacturers do not in fact give strict scientifically determined film speed ratings. They quote the ASA and DIN *meter settings* that they calculate will give optimum exposure. When using a new type of film, you should make some test exposures to discover whether the manufacturers meter settings give optimum results with your equipment. The figure you finally use should take account not only of the operation of your camera and exposure meter, but also of your preferences for negatives or transparencies of a particular density. You may have to use different settings in different conditions. For example, CdS meters tend to over-react to tungsten lighting and in such light a slightly lower meter setting may produce more satisfactory results.

Processing variations

The optimum meter setting is influenced by the processing which is anticipated. Many films can be specially processed to enable a higher setting to be used, but such processing almost always results in some loss of image quality. Black-and-white films may be processed in special fine-grain developers which necessitate the use of a lower meter setting. Using specific processing times to give you the contrast you want may also necessitate using a different film speed.

Black-and-white films

The vast majority of black-and-white films are processed to produce negatives. They consist of an emulsion of silver halides in gelatin, coated on a transparent flexible base. When this is exposed correctly, it forms an invisible *latent* image. During development the visible image of silver particles forms. The silver is deposited in proportion to the light which was focused on the film from the subject. Thus the negative is dark where the subject was light, and vice versa. When a print is made from a negative, silver is deposited in the print emulsion in proportion to the light passing through the negative and thus depicts the tones of the original subject. The characteristics of a negative depend on the type of film used, and on the processing it is given.

Grain

When a negative is magnified, it is possible to see the clumps of silver grains that form the image. This is called the grain or graininess of the negative and is proportional to the film speed; that is, the faster a film, the greater will be its grain. The grain is also influenced by the exposure and processing used. Any deviation from the normal recommendations for the film and developer—especially over-exposing or over-developing—is likely to lead to increased grain.

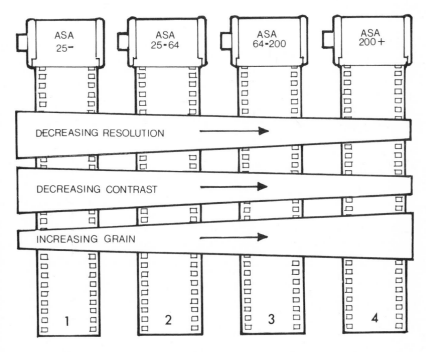

Generally speaking, films of low sensitivity to light are formed from smaller and more evenly spaced silver halide grains. Thus, the slower the film, the less noticeable the granular structure on enlargement and the higher the resolution. Common uses are: 1, very slow films, fine copying work. 2, slow films, static or brilliantly lit subjects. 3, medium speed, average photography. 4, fast, low-light photography.

Contrast

The range of grey tones a film can produce between black and white is called its contrast. Extremely high contrast materials record most of a subject as either black or white, whereas low contrast materials can give a wide range of greys between the two extremes. Normal camera films all have an acceptable contrast for general pictorial use, although the more contrasty ones give less highlight and shadow detail in pictures of high contrast subjects. As a rule, the faster a film, the lower its contrast. Prolonging the processing increases the contrast at the expense of increasing the grain.

Colour sensitivity

Untreated silver halides are sensitive only to blue light (and ultraviolet radiation). Modern photographic emulsions incorporate dyes which make them sensitive to other colours. General-purpose camera films have a sensitivity roughly the same as the human eye—and are designated *panchromatic*. High speed films have an extended red sensitivity, and some specialised emulsions are sensitive either only to blue, or to blue and green. The latter are called *orthochromatic*. The reaction of a film to different colours can be altered by the use of filters.

Exposure latitude

The best negatives are produced when the film is given the optimum exposure. However, errors of up to one stop make little difference, and printable negatives can be produced with exposures up to three stops away from the ideal, but such negatives are more difficult to print. They also have little shadow detail, if they are underexposed, or little highlight detail if they are overexposed — nor do they give as good enlargements as correctly exposed negatives. Deviation from normal processing recommendations may alter the effective speed, and special processing may be used to "retrieve" drastically mis-exposed films. It does not, however, give excellent results.

Other characteristics

Film manufacturers refer to the *acutance* or edge sharpness and *resolving power* of their films. These are two characteristics which affect the sharpness of a photographic image, but all modern films produce so sharp an image that they are characteristics of interest only in specialist applications. All modern general-purpose films also carry an anti-halation backing to prevent light that has passed through the emulsion being reflected back and degrading the image.

Choice of film

The contrast and graininess of a negative determine the degree to which the image can be enlarged. For most purposes a medium speed film (80–160 ASA, 20–23 DIN) will prove ideal. Carefully processed 35 mm negatives can yield virtually grain-free prints up to 15 × 12 inches. Slow films (20–40 ASA, 11–14 DIN) are best if you need big enlargements, and fast films 400–500 ASA, 27–28 DIN) are needed for dull conditions or fast action photography. Films faster than this (or special processing for extra speed) usually give unacceptably grainy images, and should be avoided except when there is no alternative.

Colour films

There are two types of colour film in common use—negative and reversal. Negative films are processed to produce images which are reversed in both colour and tone from the original subject. These are then used to produce colour prints. Reversal films are processed to produce a positive image closely resembling the original subject. The image is viewed either by transmitted light or projected on to a screen.

How they work
When a colour film is exposed, it produces a latent image in the same way as a black-and-white film. During processing, this is converted to a coloured dye image, the dyes being formed together with silver grains. The silver is then removed to leave the coloured dyes. In a colour negative film, the dyes correspond to the silver formed from the original latent image. They are designed also to be of complementary (opposite) colours to the original subject. In a reversal film, the original latent image is developed, and the film then re-exposed to light. On re-development, coloured dyes are produced only when (and where) the second image develops.

Exposure latitude
Just like black-and-white films, colour films must be given the right exposure. This is particularly important for reversal films, because there is no intermediate printing stage. The density of the final transparency is determined by the exposure in the

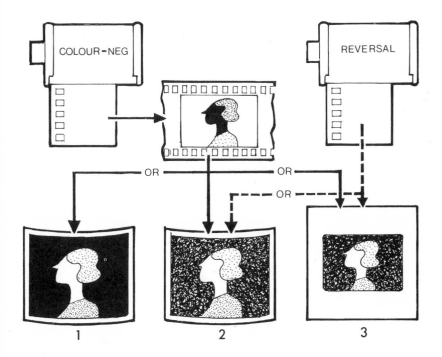

Colour negative film is for colour prints (2) but colour slides (3) or black-and-white prints (1) can be made. Colour reversal film is for slides but can be used for prints, too.

The colour pictures

The reason for having any camera is to take pictures. You can follow all the advice you can get, adorn your Nikkormat with super accessories, get perfectly exposed sharp photographs every time; yet never take a really good picture. In colour or black-and-white, with a Nikkormat or Box Brownie, it is the picture you compose in the viewfinder that matters most. Try to see the scene on your viewfinder screen as a picture—avoid concentrating just on your main subject. With colour films, be particularly careful about the range of colours you include. In this sharply lit and carefully posed portrait, the photographer has used an entirely black background to avoid distractions. You don't have to do that every time, but if you have a recognisable surround, try to make it add to the picture.

At work
Modern wide-aperture lenses and fast films let you go into every-day situations and take realistic pictures. You do have to focus carefully, though, because you have little depth of field with your lens wide open. Even with the fastest film and lens combinations, don't expect to be able to freeze any but the slowest movements.

Centre-jour
Outdoors, your problem is often too much light, particularly when you are photographing against it. If you choose shutter speed and aperture so that your main subject is properly exposed, the background tends to be too bright. You need a compromise. The girl with her two dogs has been given just enough exposure to give some detail, yet the sea and sky are still recognisable.

Interiors
Often indoor lighting is difficult. Any windows or light sources over expose heavily, while shadows just come out black. The church interior has avoided most of these problems. The photographer has allowed the distant altar to go just out of focus, so adding to the aura of size and majesty. You need a wide-angle lens (24 or 28 mm) to be at ease even in large interiors.

Fisheye Lens

The 16 mm f3.5 fisheye lens with its strong barrel distortion allows enormous depth of field. Coupled with its extremely wide angle, it lets you distort the relationships between different parts of the scene. This has made the little girl appear to dominate her father. Ultra-wide angle lenses have the same 'distorting' effects, but reproduce straight lines as straight lines.

Long Lenses

If you want to photograph animals, even in the zoo, you need a long-focus lens. The Owl was taken with an 80 to 210 mm 84.5 zoom lens, set near its longest focal length. This is a zoo picture, but careful positioning, coupled with wide aperture has hidden the bars and cages.

Close-up

The 55 mm f3.5 Micro-Nikkor is a nice lens to have on your camera in the garden. Go in close and you find a profusion of subjects. Careful focusing and a rigid support lets you get pin-sharp pictures, like the apples.

camera, which for optimum results should be correct to within half a stop. Colour negative films can produce adequate colour representation if over exposed up to two stops, or underexposed one stop. Film manufacturers supply meter settings (ASA and DIN ratings) for colour films. These will give normal results but, like any other exposure recommendation, should be modified to suit your equipment and viewing preferences.

Colour of lighting
Lighting varies greatly in colour, from the almost red light of an open fire to the strong blue of a blue sky (without sunlight). Normal daylight is a mixture of blue skylight and yellow sunlight. Our eyes adapt to the colour of lighting, but colour films do not. Compensation can be made when printing from colour negatives, but transparency films must be balanced for the light source in use. Manufacturers produce different types: Daylight—for use in daylight and with electronic flash or blue flashbulbs; Tungsten, Type A—for photolamps (3400 K) and Type B for use with studio lamps or tungsten halogen lamps (3200 K). A white object lit by a 60 watt bulb and and pictured on a daylight type film comes out a bright orange colour; whereas lit by daylight it comes out blue on a tungsten light film. Filters are available to provide correct colour balance when using a film in lighting other than that for which it is balanced.

Film speeds and image qualities
As their speed rises, colour films increase in graininess, while decreasing in contrast and colour saturation. The change in graininess and contrast being more marked than it is on black-and-white films for the same change in film speeds. Because the grain is multi-coloured, it may be considered more objectionable than that on black-and-white photographs. All commonly available colour negative films are of moderate speed (64–100 ASA, 19–21 DIN), and give results comparable with medium speed black-and-white films. Transparency films are available in slow (20–32 ASA, 14–16 DIN), moderate (64–100 ASA, 19–21 DIN) and fast (160–200 ASA, 23–24 DIN). Faster films and special processing should be reserved for cases of necessity. Many photographers use the slowest possible transparency films to give them the greatest colour saturation and sharpest images. This is particularly important if any of the pictures are to be offered for reproduction. The fast films have a distinguishable grain, but this is not noticeable at normal projection distances.

Choice of film type
Apart from the choice of (reversal) film speed, one must choose between reversal and negative films for any particular use.

Colour transparencies are ideal for group viewing, and projected images are more closely comparable to the original than are prints. They are also suitable for use as originals for photomechanical reproduction. The finest colour prints can be made from transparencies, but they are extremely expensive. Conventional colour prints made from transparencies, however, are not usually as good as those made from colour negatives.

Colour negatives can be printed directly to give either prints or transparencies of equal quality. Negative films are thus the first choice for making prints or when the final form is undecided. The main disadvantage of negative films is the cost of printing. This can be significantly reduced, however, by making (or having made) only those prints you want to keep. A number of laboratories will process a film and return it with a contact sheet so that you can select the negatives before any prints are made.

Colour temperature

Films may be exposed to any light source, and—provided that they receive the correct exposure—will produce an image. Whatever the source, black-and-white films normally produce a satisfactory picture, but colour films require more carefully selected sources. The most important quality of a light source for colour photography is its colour. Everyday light varies from strong orange produced by household tungsten lamps to the pronounced blue of a clear blue sky—such as illuminates subjects in the shadow on a sunny day. Our eyes can compensate for different colours of overall lighting: we see white objects as white with any normal light source. Colour films, however, cannot compensate, and the colour balance of pictures is influenced by the colour of the light source.

The colour quality of light may be defined as its colour temperature. This is achieved by referring to the colour of light radiated by a theoretically perfect radiator heated to any particular temperature, which is measured in kelvins (K). Thus a light source radiating light of the same quality as the radiator at 5000 K is said to have a colour temperature of 5000 K. Low colour temperature (e.g. 2500 K) indicates a yellow or orange colour, and high colour temperature (e.g. 10000 K) a blue colour.

Colour films

Colour films are balanced for particular light sources. Unless they are used with the right source, or the correct filter is used, they will not give a normal colour balance. For most purposes this is important only with reversal films—the colour balance of negatives can be corrected at the printing stage. Three types of reversal film are in common use: Daylight; type A, for use with 3400 K photolamps (over-run lamps such as Photofloods); and type B for use with 3200 K studio lamps or tungsten halogen lamps. Daylight type film is suitable for use with electronic flash (although a pale yellow filter is desirable with some units) and with blue coated flashbulbs.

Colour temperatures of some light sources

Light source	Colour temperature (K)
Skylight	12000–18000
Overcast sky	8000
Photographic 'white flame' carbon arc	7400
World average daylight	6500
Sunlight (noon)	5400
Daylight (sky and sun)	5500
English standard daylight	4800
Electronic flash	5500–7000
Blue coated flashbulb	5300
Flashcube and Magicube	4950
Low temperature carbon arc	4000
Clear flashbulb (aluminium filled)	3800
Photolamp 3400 K	3400
Tungsten studio lamp	3200
*Tungsten halogen lamp	3200
1000 watt & 500 watt floods	3000
General service bulb 200 watt	3000
General service bulb 100 watt	2900

*Photographic Studio type—others are variable

Fluorescent light sources do not always produce a continuous spectrum (i.e. light of all colours may not be equally represented), and give unpredictable results with colour films. After careful tests specially made "colour matching" tubes may prove satisfactory, but normal general service tubes are unlikely to give good pictures. When their use is unavoidable, a rough guide is to use daylight film and a red filter of the type designed for colour printing (about a 40R) with cold white tubes, and to use type B film (no filter) with warm white tubes.

The only way of ensuring accurate colour pictures when using an unknown combination of film and light source is to make a series of test exposures. For such a purpose you need a complete set of pale coloured filters—which must be of optical quality. Such filters are usually of real value only to the professional photographer.

Do not, however, be overcautious in matching even transparency films to light sources. For example, although you should use a pale blue filter, you can get quite acceptable results using unfiltered type B films with household lamps. In fact, some people prefer the warmer flesh-tones produced by this technique to correct colours. Slight over-exposure tends to minimize colour imbalance by lightening the overall density.

Mixed light sources

One very important factor, if you are to obtain an even colour balance overall, is to ensure that all the lighting used in one picture is the same colour temperature. This is just as important for colour negative films as it is for transparency films, because the colour balance of one part of a picture cannot be altered without altering the rest. The normal rule of thumb is that light sources should not differ in colour temperature by more than 100 K. Studio photographers use large pieces of filter in front of lights if they want to alter colour temperature. This is beyond most other photographers, but the use of small filters over electronic flash tubes can solve some problems. For example, using type A film an electronic flash could be mixed with photolamp (3400 K) illumination if the requisite (type A film used in daylight) filter were fitted over the flash head.

Lighting principles

With modern lenses and films, special photographic lighting is rarely necessary and there are innumerable photographers who never use any form of additional lighting.

Nevertheless, there are occasions when a specific task is made easier by arranging the subject to be photographed under controllable light sources. It is, therefore, as well to know what the conventions are.

Key light
Most subjects have form and shape and many have texture that needs to be shown. To convey form and shape, you need to arrange the lighting so that shadows are thrown in conventional way. With most objects, this means that the main or most powerful light (often call the key light) is positioned to one side up to 45° from the camera-subject axis and perhaps slightly above the subject. For spheres, faces, cubes, boxes, etc. such a single light is sufficient to indicate that the subject is three-dimensional and in most cases to show its actual shape, because shadows appear on the side of the subject farther away from the light.

Fill light
The shadows are generally very deep compared with the fully lighted parts so it is customary to add a fill light at or near the camera position. If the fill light is made about one-quarter of the intensity (on the subject) of the main light, the film is generally able to produce adequate detail in the shadows where necessary and overall

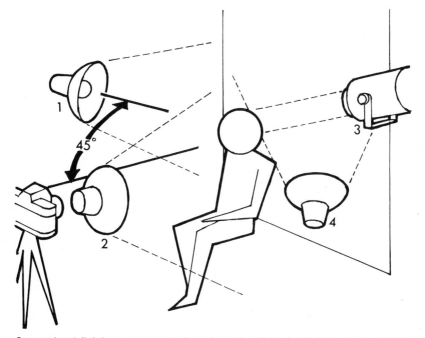

Conventional lighting arrangement. 1, main or key light. 2, fill light. 3, effect light. 4, background light.

contrast is lowered to a more acceptable level. For colour work a fill light of half the intensity of the main light may be preferable.

Effect light

These two lights can convey an effective impression of form and shape of virtually any subject but there may be subjects that need additional lighting to emphasise a particular feature. In formal portraits, for example, it is common practice to add a light to bring sparkle to the hair. This is generally a carefully directed spotlight, shielded so that its light does not spill over on to other parts of the picture. It is generally placed high up and may shine from front, back or side. This is an effect light. It might similarly be used to add a highlight to pottery, polished wood, metal objects, etc.

Background light

The only other commonly used light is the background light. It can take many forms, from simple even illumination to provide accurate colour rendering, to special effects with spots, screens and shadow masks.

These are the basic lights and their common uses but there are, of course, many ways in which they can be arranged for special effects. Where the texture of a subject—a piece of material for example—must be conveyed, the main light must be very low and directed across the surface of the material. The less the angle between the lamp beam and the surface, the more marked the texture effect becomes. In such cases, fill light where used must be kept as weak as possible.

Such shallow angle lighting can also convey mood in portraits as in the now rather hackneyed underlit effect of the horror shot.

It is always the main or key light that is moved to provide the major effect. The other lights continue to perform their functions of fill-in, special effect or background illumination. Back lighting is not uncommon, for example, to give translucent or rim-lighting effects where the light creeps round the edge of the subject. Most such shots, however, still require fill lighting from the front.

Lighting units

Many types of lighting unit are available, from simple clip-on spun metal reflector bowls and troughs of various sizes to elaborately constructed lensed spotlights. They can take either single lamps or clusters. The lamps themselves can be of the overrun type with a short life but high light output. They are generally no bigger than a small household lamp. Studio lamps on the other hand have a much longer life, consume a very heavy current, and are considerably more expensive.

Using flash

Many modern cameras have an accessory shoe mounted on the pentaprism with a centre flash contact. A cableless flashgun can fit directly into the shoe and make contact with the flash switch linked to the shutter blind movement. Cameras with no built-in accessory shoe can usually be fitted with an attachable type. The flashgun is then plugged in to the appropriate flash socket on the camera.

A flashgun on the camera does not, however, provide a very satisfactory lighting arrangement. It throws harsh shadows on nearby backgrounds and possibly under the nose, chin, hairline, etc. according to the camera position. It provides little or no modelling to features.

A simple solution to these problems is to tilt the flashgun upward or sideways to reflect light back on to the subject from a large surface, which must be white or neutral-coloured if you use colour film. Special accessories for tilting camera-mounted flash units can be obtained from photo dealers.

Whenever possible, it is better to remove the flash unit from the camera and place it to one side on an extension lead. This serves the dual purpose of separating the shadow from the subject, perhaps allowing it to be excluded from the picture area, and at the same time giving some modelling to the features by a greater variation of light and shade.

Using a second flash

Even when off the camera, however, the single flash still throws heavy shadows and, when placed for the best modelling effect, may leave parts of the subject in almost complete shadow. Such shadows can be relieved by placing a reflecting surface, such as a large card, on the other side of the subject so as to throw light back on to it or by using a second flashgun or extension head, where available, at the camera position.

The second flash should be weaker than that used for modelling because its function is to lighten the shadows slightly, not to obliterate them. It should, therefore, be farther away than the main light or should be covered by a layer or two of clean handkerchief. The second flash (plugged into a Y-connector) should preferably be of the same make and model as the first, and the method is not fully recommended owing to the possibility of overloading the flash contacts in the camera. Flash manufacturers can usually supply slave sensors which give the second flash automatically on receiving light from the first.

Flash can also be used as a fill-light in daylight, particularly to relieve the shadows thrown by an unclouded sun. You should preferably take your subject into the shade but where that is not possible, shadows thrown by back or side lighting from the sun can be relieved by a weak frontal flash. When using flash in this way, the guide number for exposure purposes should be at least doubled.

The guide number has to be modified for bounced flash too. The effective flash distance is from flash to reflecting surface and thence to the subject. There may be losses by absorption at the reflecting surface, but these are generally offset by some direct light reaching the subject from the edge of the flash beam.

Where two flashguns or an extension head are used, it is not usually necessary to take any account for exposure of the fill-in flash.

Flash equipment

The flashbulb is a glass envelope filled with finely shredded metal or metal foil in an atmosphere of oxygen. Two electrodes (wires) pass through the glass to form contacts outside the envelope to which a voltage can be applied. Current passes through the wires to a primer paste at their other ends (inside the envelope). The current causes the paste to ignite, so firing the metal filling which burns rapidly in an intense flash of light. A great deal of heat is generated and the glass envelope is shattered. The pieces are, however, held together by a heavy varnish on the outside of the envelope.

Flashgun circuitry
Flashbulbs can be fired by very low voltages but they need a high current. The average low-voltage battery could provide this high current reliably only for a very few firings. Consequently, bulb flashguns usually have a capacitor in their power circuit to act as a current store. When a suitable capacitor is connected to a battery, it rapidly charges up to the battery voltage with a relatively low current flow. When the capacitor terminals are connected to a flashbulb, they are effectively short circuited and the capacitor discharges almost instantaneously with a high current flow. While you change the bulb the capacitor charges up again.

Thus, reliability is improved and the necessary high current is always available while the battery lasts.

The flashbulb is, of course, expendable. It can be fired only once. But it comes in many sizes, from tiny bulbs like the AG-3B to the light-bulb sized monsters such as the PF100, with an output more than 12× greater. The very large bulbs generally have a screw fitting and need to be fired from a larger flashgun but small, pocketable units are adequate for several of the smaller sizes up to the PF5, which has more than double the power of the AG-3B, or special focal plane bulbs such as the PF6.

Bulb flashguns are inexpensive and can be extremely small, with folding reflectors and miniature components, the power unit consisting only of a small battery, capacitor and resistor.

All small flashbulbs are now blue-coated to simulate daylight so that they can be used with daylight colour film. Clear types are available in the larger sizes and are sometimes preferred for negative colour and black-and-white work.

The most significant difference between the flashbulb and the electronic flash tube is that the bulb takes a measurable time to ignite, needing, on average, about 20 milliseconds to reach full brilliance. The usable output of light lasts for 10–20 milliseconds, except with special long-burning focal plane bulbs designed for use with focal plane shutters at the faster speeds.

Synchronisation
The ordinary bulb can be used only at the slower speeds of a focal plane shutter because it is only at those speeds that the film is totally uncovered. At faster speeds the shutter blinds uncover only part of the film at any given moment so that the effect is of a slit travelling across the film. Only the special focal plane bulbs burn long enough to provide even illumination throughout the travel of the shutter blinds.

On all modern cameras, the firing of the flashbulb is synchronised with the shutter opening by contacts in the camera connected to a coaxial socket on the camera body and/or a contact in the accessory shoe (the "hot shoe" contact). All flashguns are provided with a cord to plug into the coaxial (PC) socket, while many have the additional hot shoe contact that needs no cord. Adapters are available to allow cord-only guns to be used on cameras with only a hot-shoe contact.

How electronic flash works

Electronic flash is basically a spark discharge between two electrodes. It relies on the fact that if two electrical conductors are brought close together and a voltage is applied to one of them, current will flow between the two conductors via a spark. Such a simple spark gives very little light, however, so for electronic flash the electrode ends are sealed into a glass tube filled with a suitable gas (usually xenon). A third electrode clamped or wound round the outside of the tube carries a very high current which ionises the gas and lowers its resistance to the spark discharge. By this means the spark can be lengthened and its brilliance enormously enhanced.

Electronic flash tubes are available in a wide variety of shapes and sizes to suit various designs of equipment from the low-power pocketable unit to the large floor-mounted equipment of the professional studio.

The weight and bulk of an electronic flash unit is governed principally by its power unit. The greater the light output required, the bigger and bulkier the power unit, which is basically similar to that of the bulb flashgun but is much more complicated because high voltages are required to fire an electronic flash tube. The trigger voltage needed to ionise the gases in the tube runs to thousands of volts while few tubes need less than 500 volts applied to the internal electrodes.

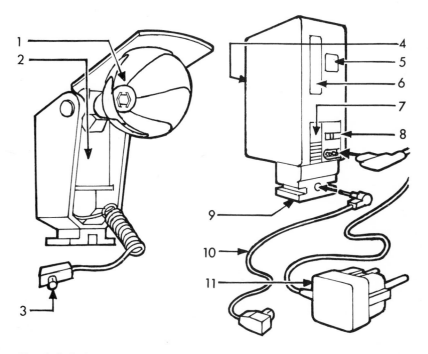

Most bulb flashguns are now very small with folding reflectors. 1, reflector. 2, battery compartment. 3, connecting cable and plug. There are also many relatively small electronic units. 4, flash tube. 5, film speed setting. 6, exposure calculator. 7, ready light. 8, power switch. 9, accessory shoe fitting. 10, connecting cable and plug. 11, charging unit.

Nevertheless the now commonly used transistor circuitry allows small electronic flashguns to operate from built-in rechargeable batteries of 1–1.5 volts. Others use two or four small dry batteries of the traditional type or the newer, high-capacity alkaline type. Many flashguns are also available with the additional facility of working from household current.

The main advantage of electronic flash is that the tube will fire thousands of times before burning out. So no bulb changing is necessary and the cost per flash is minimal over the life of the equipment. The disadvantage is that, weight for weight, the bulb flash can be considerably more powerful. An electronic flash unit able to provide a light output equivalent to that of, say, a PF5, would be very bulky indeed, while nothing short of a really heavy floor-mounted power unit could provide anything approaching the output of the largest flashbulbs.

Nevertheless, even the smaller electronic units can be sufficiently powerful for a variety of uses and they have the added advantage of controllability that comes with automatic operation in the latest models.

Automatic or "computer" flash

The guide number system of flash exposure calculation calls for a certain agility with figures that many people find irksome. Even the calculator discs incorporated in most small electronic flashguns made the necessary calculations only slightly easier. Various semi-automatic methods have been tried by camera manufacturers but the only really simple and fully automatic method applied to the flashgun itself is that of the so-called computer type. The word is here used in its normal sense in that the flash unit circuitry calculates the amount of light needed in given circumstances and terminates the output from the flash tube when that amount of light has been emitted from the tube.

Basically, the procedure is that the light reflects back from the subject to a sensor in the flashgun which, with its allied circuitry, measures the amount of light and switches off the tube when the correct amount of light has been received. Naturally, such units can operate only within the range of their available light output and must be pre-set to take account of the speed of the film in the camera. This is usually achieved by allocating one lens aperture value (f-number) or a limited range of f-numbers for use with each film speed. On a typical small unit, for example, the lens aperture must be set to f 8 or f 5.6 when using a 125 ASA film. A switch on the flashgun is moved to the appropriate position for either of these settings and a third position allows the unit to be used manually in the normal way.

Disadvantages of these units are that they should generally be mounted on or very near to the camera and few of them allow indirect lighting because the light measured by the sensor would in that case be the light from the reflecting surface used to provide the indirect lighting. There are a few units, however, which allow the head to be swivelled independently of the sensor, which can still point at the subject. Again, however, as the sensor should remain close to the camera, the value of such units is limited. Some units can be connected to a separate sensor mounted on the camera.

There are two types of automatic flashgun. In the earlier models, the light not used was diverted through a so-called black tube and was wasted. In later models, this unused power is returned to the power unit capacitor, providing the twin advantages of more flashes per set of batteries or battery recharge and a faster recycling time. Naturally, however, these advantages are considerable only if you carry out a large proportion of ultra close range work calling for short exposures. With colour materials in particular, such methods are not advisable, owing to the possible effects of reciprocity failure.

Flash exposures

Unlike other light sources, a flashbulb or single firing of an electronic flash tube emit a finite, constant and measurable amount of light. In general use the flash is also small enough to be regarded as a point light source, which means that it is subject to the inverse square law—the amount of light reaching the subject is in inverse proportion to the ratio between the squares of the flash-to-subject distances. With the flash at 9 ft the light on the subject is $(3/9)^2$ or one-ninth the strength of the same flash at 3 ft from the subject.

Lens apertures work in a similar way. At $f2$ the light transmitted is $(8/2)^2$ or 16 times the light transmitted at $f8$.

Thus, whenever flash distance and f-number multiplied together give the same result the amount of light reaching the film is the same, i.e. $f2$ and 20 ft, $f4$ and 10 ft, $f8$ and 5 ft etc., because, for example, changing from $f4$ to $f2$ *increases* light transmission fourfold while changing the flash distance from 10 ft to 20 ft *decreases* the light falling on the subject fourfold.

If these factors provided correct exposure, therefore the figure 40 could be ascribed to that particular flash unit as an exposure guide number.

That is how the guide number system works. Every flashbulb and electronic flash unit has guide numbers applicable to various film speeds. Flashbulb packings also quote different guide numbers according to shutter speed but these do not normally apply to focal plane shutters, with which the faster speeds cannot be used. You take the open flash or 1/30 sec number. When using focal plane type bulbs, you should use the guide number for your chosen shutter speed.

To calculate the aperture required for correct exposure, you simply divide the flash distance (not the camera distance, unless the flash is on the camera) into the guide number and round off to the nearest f-number. Alternatively, if you wish to shoot at a particular aperture you divide the f-number into the guide number to find the distance at which you have to place the flash.

If that means that the flash has to be used at a greater distance than that from which you wish to shoot, you can use an extension flash cable, obtainable from any photo dealer.

Typical flash guide numbers (feet/metres)

Flash source	Film speeds (ASA)				
	25–40	50–80	100–160	200–320	400–640
MF Class bulbs					
Small bulbs, magicubes					
flashcubes (Type 1B,					
AG1B, AG3B etc)	60/18	80/24	120/36	160/48	240/72
Medium (Type 5B etc)	100/30	160/48	200/60	320/96	400/120
FP-Class bulbs					
Medium (Type 6B etc)	45/14	65/20	90/27	130/39	180/54
Electronic flash					
Small pocket guns	25/8	40/12	50/15	80/24	100/30
Medium pocket guns	40/12	60/18	80/24	120/36	160/48
Large 'pocket' guns	50/15	70/21	100/30	140/142	200/60
'Professional' type guns	70/21	100/30	140/42	200/60	280/76

Guide numbers for bulbs apply only to shutter speeds of 1/30 second or longer (1/60 with FP bulbs). At shorter speeds the number must be reduced.
Electronic flash guide numbers apply at all suitable speeds.

Filters and screens

Filters for mounting on camera lenses must be of the highest optical quality. There is no point in buying a specially coated lens accurately made from selected high quality glasses and then fitting over it a filter little better than a piece of window glass. Optical quality gelatin filters are ideal for occasional use, but are too delicate to be used continuously. For constant use glass filters (often a gelatin filter cemented between two pieces of glass) are essential. Filters manufactured for fitting over light sources (either photographic or theatrical) or in colour enlarger heads may produce distorted or degraded pictures if used on the camera. Intentional distortion may be introduced by using a dirty filter, or specially constructed lens attachments and screens. By such means, you can produce blurred images, flare, stars from bright points, multiple images and many other effects. Together with brightly coloured filters, these attachments play an important part in creative photography, but care should be taken to avoid accidentally emulating their effects. You should be specially careful of the condition and quality of a UV filter if, like many photographers, you keep it permanently in place.

Glass filters are supplied in rims which screw into the filter threads on the front of the lenses. The rims are manufactured in a standard range of sizes to suit most lenses. Adapter rings are available to allow the use of larger filters on lenses with smaller filter threads. Because of the standardization, you may be able to use one filter on several lenses, thus justifying the expense of buying a top quality filter.

As filters reduce the light reaching the film, they usually necessitate an increase in exposure time (or lens aperture). This increase is given as the *factor* by which the exposure time should be increased.

Aperture alterations can be calculated from this factor. Thus, for example, a $2 \times$ filter requires twice the exposure time or one stop larger aperture etc. Some manufacturers also give exposure increases in *thirds* of a stop. The simplest way of using these with a separate exposure meter (or one built into the camera which uses its own light window) is to decrease the film speed setting by one unit for each $\frac{1}{3}$ stop. Thus a $\frac{2}{3}$ stop increase would need an alteration from 80 ASA (20 DIN) to 50 ASA (18 DIN). Cameras with built-in through-the-lens meters also read through the filter, and thus give the correct exposure without any modification to the film setting. The meter can be used in its normal way.

Filters for black-and-white film
When they are used with black-and-white films UV and polarizing filters reduce haze and reflection respectively, just as they do with colour films. Coloured filters, however, affect the relative tonal rendering of different coloured parts of the subject. Because a filter acts by reducing the passage of light of complementary (opposite) colour, it reduces the image density produced on the negative from an object of that colour. The object thus comes out darker in the final print. If—as is usually the case—the camera exposure is increased to take account of the light absorbed by the filter, objects the same colour as the filter will be rendered lighter than normal in the final print.

The complements of red, green and blue are cyan (blue-green), magenta (red-purple) and yellow respectively; intermediate colours have intermediate complements. From this you can work out the colour of filter you need to give particular emphasis to any part of the subject. Yellow filters are widely used to darken blue parts of the subjects—in particular blue skies to emphasise white clouds.

Without any filter, blue parts of a subject tend to be rendered somewhat lighter than we see them because blue light tends also to contain some ultra-violet radiation, to which the film is sensitive, and the eye is not very sensitive to blue light. For this reason, a medium yellow filter may give a more natural tone rendering on panchromatic film, and is sometimes called a correction filter. The effect may be exaggerated by using a dark yellow or orange filter, or for greatest exaggeration a red filter. Such filters give increasingly darkened skies, with clouds standing out dramatically. The accepted "correction" filter for use with tungsten light is a yellow-green colour.

Because haze tends to reflect blue light and ultra-violet radiation in preference to green or red light, the use of yellow, red or orange filters can reduce its effect on the film. Deep red filters give the strongest haze penetration, but require considerable exposure increase, and of course affect the overall tonal rendering of the photograph.

Neutral density filters, naturally, do not affect the tone rendering. They simply allow you to increase the aperture or lengthen the shutter speed without overexposing the film.

Filters for colour photography

Filters are used in colour photography to alter the colour balance of the image on the film. Their use is mainly confined to reversal films because the colour balance of a print can be determined at the printing stage. Polarizing and ultra-violet absorbing filters, however, are commonly used with negative films as well.

Polarizing filters. The effect of a polarizing filter is the same with all types of film. It can—in some circumstances—reduce reflections; and can darken a blue sky, without otherwise altering the balance in a colour picture.

Light coming directly from the sun or other light source is not polarized: the rays vibrate in all directions. Sometimes, however, light can be restricted to rays all vibrating in one plane. It is then said to be polarized. For the photographer there are two important polarizers: polarizing filters, which restrict the passage of all light not vibrating in their plane of polarization; and smooth reflective non-metallic surfaces which polarize light reflected at certain angles. Although polarizing filters may be fitted over light-sources for special applications, they can normally be regarded as camera fitments used to take advantage of light polarized by reflection.

The most common use is in restricting the passage of polarized light, thus reducing its influence on the film. From certain angles this can result in a dramatic reduction in reflections from glass, water and similar substances (but not from metal surfaces). A special instance of this is the blue light reflected from the sky on a sunny day. An area of the sky at right angles to a line from the sun to the camera position polarises the sun's rays strongly, and thus careful use of a polarizing filter can selectively darken a blue sky in a colour picture.

The effect of a polarizing filter depends on its orientation to the polarized light. It passes almost all light polarized parallel to its polarizing plane, and is opaque to light polarized at right angles.

To simplify their use, polarizing filters for camera use are usually supplied in rotatable mounts. With a single lens reflex camera, you simply view the subject and rotate the filter until you see the effect you want. Some types also have a small extra filter on the rotation handle. This allows you to check the polarizing action independently of the main filter. Polarizing filters require an exposure increase of about $2\frac{1}{2}$ times ($1\frac{1}{3}$ stops).

Ultra-violet filters. Ultra-violet absorbing (UV) filters reduce the effect of atmospheric haze which would otherwise be exaggerated because photographic emulsions are sensitive to ultra-violet radiation (which is invisible to the eye). The radiation is scattered strongly by haze and records on colour film as a blue veiling of distant objects.

117

With colour reversal film an ultra-violet filter has the same haze-cutting effect, and also reduces the blue cast sometimes found in transparencies taken close to large reflecting masses such as water or snow. Such filters require no exposure increase.

Sky-light filters. Skylight filters are ultra-violet absorbing filters coloured a pale salmon or rose. They are used with reversal films to give slightly warmer colours in transparencies, as well as the normal UV filter effects. They require no exposure increase, and are a more useful alternative to plain UV filters.

Colour conversion filters. To obtain a normal colour balance when using a colour reversal film with a light source other than that for which it is intended to be used, you must use a coloured filter. Filters designed for this purpose are known as conversion filters. Many manufacturers supply them for using commonly available film types in normal types of illumination. In general, filters for use with daylight films are blue in colour, and those for use with artificial light films are orange. The filters are normally used on the camera lens, but are equally effective when used to filter the light-source. If you are to use two light sources of different colour temperatures, one of them must be filtered to the colour of the other.

Colour balancing filters. For special effects and for accurate colour matching, it may be necessary to change the colour balance slightly. Manufacturers supply two types of filter which are suitable: special pale filters designed for the purpose, and filters designed for colour printing. Almost invariably the necessity for particular filters can be determined only by testing, and information should be sought from the filter manufacturers.

Neutral density filters. Neutral density filters (or attenuators) reduce equally the transmission of all wavelengths of the visible spectrum. They come in two forms —*photographic silver density*, which is simply accurately exposed and developed film; and *dyed filters*—often using colloidal carbon. Because of its high light-scattering effect, silver density is not suitable for use over the camera lens. Dyed neutral density filters are, however, intended for this purpose, and can be used to produce high quality images.

Neutral density filters do not affect the colour balance whatever film they are used with. They simply allow the lens aperture to be widened, or the shutter speed lengthened, while restricting the exposure to its normal level. They are normally available in a range of densities from 0.1 to 4.0 (transmitting from 80% to 0.01% of the available light) with filter factors varying from just over 1 to 10,000. A density between 1.0 and 2.0 (10%–1% transmission) enables you to use full aperture in bright sun with medium speed films. A density of 3.0 (0.1% transmission) allows exposures up to 30 sec under the same conditions.

Focusing methods

One of the few camera operations that has not yet been satisfactorily automated is the task of adjusting the lens position to provide a sharp image on the film—known slightly inaccurately as focusing the lens. It is not always a simple operation. When you have a single main subject or the whole of the subject is more or less in the same plane, there is no problem, but many subjects occupy some depth in space (as in landscapes) and the focus has to be placed with some care. When, for example, the landscape has the classic open gate in the foreground to lead the eye into the picture and out to the line of hills beyond, you do not focus on either the gate or the hills. You have to choose an aperture and focused distance to give you the depth of field required. If any sacrifice in sharpness is to be made it should usually be in the background rather than the foreground. A similar principle applies to almost any subject in depth. The usual advice is to focus at a point about one-third into the zone required to be sharp but it is generally easier to set the distance of your farthest required sharp plane to the "far" aperture number at which you are shooting on the depth of field scale (or preferably at one stop larger). Then check that the depth of field provided is adequate to cover the nearest required plane.

With reflex cameras you can, of course, check the screen image by using the depth of field preview button, but screen texture does tend to sharpen the image and at small apertures it is not easily seen.

Action and movement

Focusing a moving object can raise problems because the delay between focusing and shooting can result in the subject moving well out of focus again.

When the subject is moving within or can be confined to, a reasonably restricted area, the technique of zone focusing is useful. This makes use of depth of field again. You set your lens to the smallest practicable aperture and set the lens distance scale to a mid-point that allows the depth of field to cover the required zone. A football photographer, for example, might wish to cover action within the penalty area from behind the goal. If he focuses on 20 ft at $f8$ with a 50 mm lens he will just about cover that zone. You can work out your own zones for your own purposes by consulting depth of field tables or the indicator on your lens.

Objects that move in a predictable direction, such as racing cars, athletes, etc., are more easily dealt with by focusing on a spot that the subject has to pass and releasing the shutter as the spot is reached. A sports or frame finder is a useful accessory for such shots to enable you to keep your eye on the subject before it reaches the selected spot.

Depth of field

In theory, a lens placed at a given distance from the image plane (the film) produces a sharp image of objects in a single plane at a certain distance in front of the lens. Objects in front of or behind that plane are rendered less sharply.

In practice, each image point formed by a lens is, in fact, a disc of finite size and, up to a certain degree of enlargement for a given viewing distance, the difference between the smallest possible disc and various slightly larger discs is indistinguishable to the human eye. The relative sizes of the various discs or image points formed by a lens can be envisaged by regarding the light reflected from the point and concentrated by the lens as a solid cone, with the effective aperture of the lens as its base. Thus, when the aperture is small and/or the lens-to-subject distance is large, the cone is relatively slender. At its apex (the crossover point for objects behind the focused plane), there is a relatively deep zone both fore and aft in which the discs formed by a section through the cone are still small enough to be rendered as discs indistinguishable from points on the film and, indeed, on considerably enlarged images.

This zone is the depth of field. As our explanation implies, it is greater when the effective lens aperture is smaller and when the focused distance is greater.

Enlargement and viewing distance

A complication arises with the comparatively small negative or slide sizes used today. Most final images, whether prints or projected slides, are considerably larger than the images produced on the film. Moreover, many prints are made from only part of the negative image and the degree of enlargement is not proportional to the print size. But most final images are viewed from a distance appropriate to their size, not, as they ideally should be, to their degree of enlargement. The complication then is that detail which looks sharp when enlarged less or viewed from a greater distance looks distinctly less sharp when enlarged to a greater degree or viewed from closer range.

Depth of field formulae and tables, therefore, must always be regarded as approximations. Although it is possible to make exact mathematical calculations based on focal length, f-number, focused distance and the size of the acceptable disc (known in this context as the circle of confusion), it is self-evident that you do not produce a sharp image of an object at 10.1 metres and an unsharp image of an object at 10.11 or even 10.2 metres. Depending on the use you wish to make of depth of field or the lack of it, you should always use at least a stop smaller or larger than calculators, indicators or tables recommend.

Changing the focused distance

In many cases, you can manipulate depth of field by changing your focused distance. When you want to throw the background out of focus, for example, you can focus forward a little, so that the subject is within the depth of field but the background is well behind it. The opposite also applies. If you focus slightly beyond the subject you extend the zone of sharpness behind it.

When you wish to obtain the greatest depth of field at any given aperture you set the focus at the hyperfocal distance for that aperture. This distance can be calculated or looked up in tables but the easiest method is to set the lens distance scale so that the infinity marking is opposite the f-number at which you are shooting on the depth of field scale. You are then focused at the hyperfocal distance and the depth of field stretches from half that distance to infinity.

Shooting at close range

To enable a lens to focus objects close to it, the distance between the film and the lens needs to be increased. That is what you do when you turn the focusing ring on the average lens. The glass components of the lens move forward in their mounting within the lens barrel. With most lenses the amount of travel thus provided is restricted and the closest focus allowed with the average standard lens barely reaches the true close-up field. A wide angle lens generally focuses closer, while the longer the focal length the more distant the minimum focusing plane.

If you wish to focus at really close range, therefore, you have two alternatives:

1. You can add a lens to the camera lens to shorten its focal length so that the existing travel has a greater effect.
2. You can interpose extension tubes or an extension bellows between lens and camera to increase the separation between camera and film.

Close-up lenses

Close-up lenses are relatively inexpensive, usually single-glass constructions in filter-type mounts to attach to the front of the camera lens. They are rated in dioptres, indirectly indicating the focal length, which is the dioptre number divided into one metre. Thus a 1-dioptre lens has a focal length of one metre or $39\frac{1}{4}$ in; the focal length of a 3-dioptre lens is 30 cm or about 13 in. Strengths above 3 dioptres are less common and generally need to be of higher quality and price.

With the camera lens set to infinity you can focus objects at a distance equal to the focal length of the close-up lens, measured from the front of the lens. The normal focusing travel allows a restricted range of closer focusing.

Exposure is not affected by the close-up lens. There is no increase in lens extension so the aperture values remain as in normal photography.

Extension tubes and bellows

Extension tubes are, exactly as their name implies, metal rings or tubes to provide a fixed amount of additional distance between lens and film. They are usually supplied in sets of three, typical values being 7, 14 and 28 mm. Automatic types are now available for most reflex cameras, connecting the auto-diaphragm mechanisms of camera body and lens.

Extension bellows perform the same function but allow variable extension between the limits of the bellows length and the minimum extension provided by the front and rear standards and the fully compressed bellows. Automatic diaphragm facilities are not generally available with bellows except by an external linkage or the use of a double cable release.

Exposure factors

As the function of extension tubes and bellows is to increase the distance between lens and film and therefore the distance the image-forming rays have to travel, there is a loss of light intensity at the film surface. This means that the lens f-numbers do not give an accurate impression of the exposure effect. Rather than adjust the f-number for each degree of extension, however, it is easier to use an exposure factor calculated from $(E/F)^2$, where E = total extension, i.e. focal length plus additional extension provided by bellows or tubes, and F = focal length of the camera lens. Thus, when 7 mm and 28 mm extension tubes are used together on a 50 mm lens, the exposure factor is $(85/50)^2 = 2.89$. The normally calculated exposure should thus be increased threefold, i.e. open up the lens by $1\frac{1}{2}$ stops. No such calculation is necessary, however, where the camera has a through-the-lens meter.

Close-up depth of field

Aperture	Depth of field in inches for scale of reproduction						
f	0·1 (1 : 10)	0·17 (1 : 6)	0·25 (1 : 4)	0·5 (1 : 2)	1 (1 : 1)	2 (2 : 1)	3 (3 : 1)
2	0·22	0·084	0·040	0·012	0·0040	0·0015	0·0009
2·8	0·31	0·12	0·056	0·017	0·0056	0·0021	0·0012
4	0·44	0·17	0·080	0·024	0·0080	0·0030	0·0018
5·6	0·62	0·23	0·11	0·034	0·011	0·0042	0·0025
8	0·88	0·34	0·16	0·048	0·016	0·0060	0·0036
11	1·21	0·46	0·22	0·066	0·022	0·0082	0·0049
16	1·76	0·67	0·32	0·096	0·032	0·012	0·0071
22	2·42	0·92	0·44	0·13	0·044	0·016	0·0098
32	3·5	1·34	0·64	0·19	0·064	0·024	0·014
45	4·9	1·90	0·90	0·27	0·090	0·034	0·020

Aperture	Depth of field in millimetres for scale of reproduction						
f	0·1 (1 : 10)	0·17 (1 : 6)	0·25 (1 : 4)	0·5 (1 : 2)	1 (1 : 1)	2 (2 : 1)	3 (3 : 1)
2	5·5	2·10	1·00	0·30	0·10	0·038	0·022
2·8	7·7	2·94	1·40	0·42	0·14	0·052	0·031
4	11·0	4·2	2·00	0·60	0·20	0·775	0·044
5·6	15·4	5·9	2·80	0·84	0·28	0·10	0·062
8	22·0	8·4	4·0	1·20	0·40	0·15	0·089
11	30	11·5	5·5	1·65	0·55	0·21	0·12
16	44	16·8	8·0	2·40	0·80	0·30	0·18
22	60	23·1	11·0	3·3	1·10	0·41	0·24
32	88	34	16·0	4·8	1·60	0·60	0·36
45	124	47	22·5	6·7	2·25	0·84	0·50

Circle of confusion 0·001 in/0·025 mm. The depth of field shown is at each side of the plane of sharp focus. The total depth is twice these figures.

Working methods

Important points to bear in mind when working at close range is that depth of field is extremely shallow and perspective distortion of three-dimensional objects is inevitable. You can reduce the perspective distortion by shooting from a greater distance with a longer focus lens but you can do little about the reduced depth of field beyond focusing precisely on the plane of most importance and stopping down as far as possible.

In most set-ups, a tripod is essential, because of the requirement for accurate focusing. It is quite possible to hand-hold, however, when using very little extra extension on longer focus lenses to shoot, for example, wild flowers or plants. You may well be able to use a small flashgun on such occasions and shoot at small apertures.

Tele-extenders can be used in close-range work to magnify the image without moving closer and risking perspective distortion. In static set-ups, the light loss is rarely of great importance.

Time exposures

For many years after the introduction of photography, the standard exposures were several seconds, or even minutes, long. Portraits were taken with the subjects sitting rigidly still, their heads firmly supported by a neck clamp. Today such long exposures—usually called time exposures—are necessary only in very low light levels or for special effects.

Time exposures may be needed for taking photographs indoors by the existing light, or outdoors after dark. Occasionally, under normal lighting conditions, a time exposure may be needed to allow a small lens aperture to give maximum depth of field. Very long time exposures may be used to picture a scene which would otherwise be marred by transitory objects or people. For example, as long as none of them stay still for much of the time a 30 min exposure in a public square could produce a picture devoid of any signs of people passing through. Even with a slow film, to avoid over-exposure, such a picture would require a dense neutral density filter over the camera lens. In darkened conditions, time exposures may be used to record moving lights, such as fireworks or stars, as streaks on the film.

Whenever the exposure is longer than 1/30 sec, the camera must be firmly supported, preferably on a tripod or other specially designed camera stand. Care must be taken to avoid shaking the camera, and it is best to use a cable release to trip the shutter.

The range of mechanically timed shutter speeds is limited by the construction of the shutter mechanism. You can make longer exposures by using the B (brief time or bulb) setting. On this setting, the shutter remains open as long as the shutter button is depressed. If you use a locking cable release, the shutter can be locked open at the beginning of the exposure and will not close until the cable release is unlocked. This is useful for exposures longer than half a minute, and essential—unless you can lock the shutter button down—for much longer exposures. A number of accessory manufacturers supply timers which give accurately timed exposures when used on the B setting. Some of these have a built-in delay to allow vibrations to die down.

If you can lock down the shutter button—or arrange for it to be held down with sticky tape, it is possible to use long exposure times without a cable release. The camera must be set up to take the photo and firmly supported. While the button is being pressed and locked—or stuck—down, you prevent light reaching the film by holding a matt black object just in front of the lens. The lens cap could be used, but must be positioned accurately so that it excludes all light without actually touching the lens mount. You then allow all vibrations to die away, and make the exposure by letting the light reach the lens, finishing by re-covering it. If you use the lens cap, it can now be pushed securely into place. Mechanically timed exposures, which would normally need a cable release, can be made using a self-timer (either built-in or as an accessory) to release the shutter. This allows the camera to become quite still before opening the shutter.

Exposure calculations

It is difficult to calculate the exact exposure needed because film emulsions react unusually to long exposure times. This is especially marked with colour films, many of which produce progressively worse colour balance as the exposure times increase over about one second. For optimum results, you should take several pictures "bracketing" your calculated exposure by at least two stops either way. Although your meter may well not give you the exposure time directly, you may be able to calculate it from readings taken at wider apertures, or with a higher film speed.

Interchangeable lenses

One of the major reasons for buying a system camera, particularly a single-lens reflex, is to enable you to choose the lens to suit the picture. The most important feature of a lens is its angle of view. For any given format, this is directly related to its focal length. The angle of view is normally measured across the diagonal of the format. The angles of view of normal lenses for 35 mm cameras vary from about 110° to 1°. The quoted angles of view for really short focus lenses (less than 20 mm) tend to vary from one manufacturer to another, partly because slight variations in actual focal length greatly affect the angles and partly because of differing measurement techniques. The only way to determine whether a lens is suited to your purpose is to test it on your camera.

Different focal lengths

Choosing the focal length—and thus the angle of view—of a lens allows you to choose the area of a scene you include from a particular viewpoint. Wide-angle lenses allow you to include a broad sweep in one picture, whereas long-focus (narrow-angle) lenses allow you to concentrate on one small part—thus magnifying a distant object. If you can alter your viewpoint, altering the focal length allows you to vary the perspective in your picture while still showing the important part of your subject the same size. Another reason for changing from one lens to another is to change the depth of field while maintaining a usable f-number.

Although individual photographers tend to regard other lenses as their standard, most 35 mm cameras are supplied with a lens of between 45 and 55 mm. These

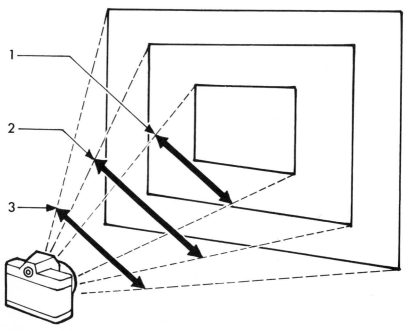

Interchangeable lenses allow more or less to be included in the picture at different ratios of reproduction. 1, long-focus. 2, standard. 3, wide-angle.

lenses approximate to the angle of view of the human eye (50–43°), and so under most circumstances produce pictures with pleasing perspective (when they are viewed from a "normal" distance). Some photographers advocate wider angles, such as 55–62° (40–35 mm), whereas others prefer to take most of their pictures with an 85 or 90 mm lens giving an angle of about 27 or 28°, so the 45–55 mm seems to be a good compromise.

Long-focus lenses

Most non-photographers immediately assume that extra lenses are telephoto lenses, because some of their attributes are obvious. They allow the user to take photos of distant subjects, or to isolate the important parts of a scene. Telephoto lenses are, in fact, long-focus lenses which have a physical length shorter than their focal length, and they behave in exactly the same way as ordinary long-focus lenses of the same focal length. They are, however, smaller and lighter.

Moderately long-focus lenses—about 85 to 150 mm—have two functions. They magnify parts of the subject too distant to be pictured with the standard lens and allow the photographer to use a viewpoint which gives pleasing perspective in portraits. These two features combine to make them excellent lenses for taking pictures of children playing or of relatively unsuspecting adults. Lenses from 80 to 105 mm are usually regarded as optimum for normal portrait work.

Longer-focus lenses are useful for sports or nature photography, as they give quite large images even when you cannot get near the subject. Because they also magnify the effects of subject or camera movement, however, they need some care in handling, and lenses longer than 300 mm focal length are unlikely to give their best performance without a firm support.

Shooting from a distance has the effect of compressing the perspective of the final picture. This is purely an effect of magnifying part of the scene, as may be seen by enlarging a small sector from a negative taken with the standard lens, but the "crowding" effect should be remembered when composing your picture. You can use the effect, for example, to picture an enormous moon apparently just behind a close-up of a tree, which was actually some distance from the camera.

Wide-angle lenses

For many photographers, the first accessory lens is a wide-angle. Wide-angle lenses for single lens reflex cameras are normally of reversed telephoto construction. This construction allows them to focus an image on the film from a distance greater than their focal length, thus allowing room for the mirror to move up and down.

The most popular wide-angle lens has long been the 35 mm, but 30 or 28 mm lenses are becoming much more widely used. Such wide angle lenses allow you to get more in a picture without moving back further, and are particularly useful when shooting in confined spaces. One particular use is to take pictures of tall buildings, without the converging verticals which would be caused if you were to tilt the camera to include the top.

The other important feature of wide-angle lenses is their great depth of field. Careful use can give pictures in which the whole subject is sharp from a few feet to infinity. Such pictures, however, often show "wide-angle distortion" because of the close viewpoint needed to picture objects at a large size. The effect is often used creatively, but wide-angle lenses—especially extreme ones of 24 mm or less—must be treated with respect if this effect is not to spoil your normal pictures.

Building up a system

A "system" camera is only the basis of a system. The ease and efficiency with which you can deal with your picture taking depends largely on the accessories you select. An important factor in such selection must be portability. It is no good attempting nature photography if you can't carry your equipment without a car!

Lenses

Accessory lenses are an essential part of any system, but they should be selected with care, taking account of how they relate to one another and what other lenses you may need later. It is also important to choose a range which you can carry with you and which covers all your likely uses.

Most cameras are supplied with a standard lens, and others should normally be chosen to complement it. The most useful wide-angle to supplement this for the 35 mm photographer is probably a 28 mm, which gives greatly increased coverage and depth of field and can be used without the special care needed with ultrawide (15–25 mm) lenses. A suitable long-focus companion to these is a 100 to 150 mm lens. If you don't intend to buy any more long focus lenses, the choice will depend only on the expected uses. A lens of around 100 mm is best for portraits, but a longer one is probably more useful for picturing distant objects. For most photographers, 125 or 135 mm is a good compromise.

If you intend to build further, your first purchases should be considered more carefully. For example if you envisage using a 200 mm lens at some later date, a 100 mm would be a better choice than a 150 mm, whereas if you were contemplating a 300 mm lens, perhaps for sports photography, a 150 mm may be a better companion. Lenses much longer than 300 mm, or much shorter than 28 mm should only be considered for specialist purposes, and may be of less influence on your choice of general purpose lenses.

If you are starting from scratch you might consider buying a camera body without a standard lens, and then a selection of lenses. Thus you might choose a 35 mm and 85 mm to start, adding perhaps a 24 mm and 150 mm at a later date. This would be a particularly valuable saving if you ever intended buying a 50 mm macro lens, which makes a perfectly good "standard" lens.

There are two major types of lenses useful for increasing your versatility: teleconverters and zooms. The major disadvantage of teleconverters is that they reduce the light reaching the film, but under daylight conditions with fast prime lenses, this may be inconsequential. For example, an expedition photographer could probably cover most situations with a 28 mm $f2.8$ and a 100 mm $f2.8$ lens if he had a 2 and 3 times converter. This would give 28 mm $f2.8$, 56 mm $f5.6$, 84 mm $f8$, 100 mm $f2.8$, 200 mm $f5.6$ and 300 mm $f8$ combinations; not particularly impressive until you remember that with one lens on the camera the rest will go in one pocket. If absolute definition is of the utmost concern, however, the prime lenses and the converter must be of the highest quality. Zoom lenses allow you to cover a range of focal lengths, but their sizes, weights and maximum apertures are governed by their longest focal length. Thus an 85–200 mm lens is a versatile substitute for a 200 mm lens, but a clumsy one for an 85 mm. If you expect to use all the range quite often, a zoom lens may be a good addition to your system. If, however, most of your work is at one end or other, you would probably be better served by a suitable prime lens—and possibly a teleconverter for the odd occasion. Both these accessories are covered in more detail in the sections on equipment for your camera.

Close-ups and special accessories
Close up equipment ranges from simple accessory lenses to microscopes. While accessory lenses are useful for the occasional job a set of extension tubes will give more versatility. To increase this further a set of extension bellows is useful but we are coming to equipment which needs a bag of its own, and if portability is the prime concern, the choice requires careful thought. Remember that it is difficult to use the full capabilities of even small bellows without a firm tripod or similar support. For many field shots, a longish lens (say 85–125 mm) with a small extension tube gives adequate image size without being a burden.

SLR cameras are simple to use on microscopes, usually with adapters supplied. However, photography is normally considered as an extension of microscopy, rather than vice versa, and a microscope would not normally be considered part of a camera system. Likewise, many astronomers—amateur and professional—use a camera with their telescopes, but the latter could not really be thought of as camera accessories.

Filters
Many photographers keep an ultra-violet absorbing filter permanently on their lenses to prevent damage. This is normally unnecessary except under hazardous conditions, and unless the filter is of superb quality, will probably reduce the absolute definition of negatives. Other filters should be considered as the occasion arises. If your lens set needs several different sizes, you may be able to economise by buying large filters and adapter rings.

Cases
Cases fall into two categories—ever-ready camera cases, lens cases etc. usually supplied by the equipment manufacturer, and gadget bags or equipment cases.

Ever-ready cases are a matter of taste—many photographers find them a nuisance, and often the best compromise is to remove the front flap and leave it at home, thus retaining some protection without inconvenience. They are, however, good for protecting the camera in storage, as are the round zip or clip up lens cases supplied with most lenses.

However, if you want to carry several items with you, the simplest way is to put them all into one case. If you carry the camera separately, a small gadget bag is very handy. The sort that are supposed to hold a camera and two accessory lenses will hold about three lenses, a small flashgun and several cassettes of film, together with filters, extension leads and other small items. For real strength, however, there is no substitute for foam-lined aluminium cases. These can be bought in a number of sizes, and have foam inserts which are cut to provide tight-fitting compartments for all your pieces of equipment. Professional photographers, who are not unduly worried about the looks of their equipment, tend to carry it loose in a leather hold-all. Whatever form your system case takes, you should leave all the individual cases behind—they take up space and get in the way. Lenses are quite safe with caps on both ends if they are kept in small polythene bags to prevent surface markings.

Camera care

So many cameras now use batteries for one purpose or another that they have become an important point in camera care. If you do not expect to use your camera for a prolonged period, remove all batteries. None of them are totally leakproof and a long period of disuse could cause them to corrode and damage the camera contacts.

With the batteries removed, store the camera away from damp and dust, preferably sealed in a plastic bag.

Ideally, no camera should be stored. The camera is designed to be used. If it is not, its mechanism can become sluggish and unreliable. If possible, operate the mechanism a few times each month even if you don't actually take any pictures. If storage is inevitable, when you take the camera out, check it over thoroughly, operating all shutter speeds several times with the lens removed or back open so that you can observe the shutter action. If you use flash, plug a flashgun in and make a few test shots, again watching for synchronisation through front or back with the lens in place.

Insert new batteries and check the exposure meter and any other battery-powered operation.

Cleaning operations

In normal use, the camera needs little attention. The best treatment, in fact, to keep it in good condition is constant use. Avoid any cleaning operation unless it is absolutely essential. A few specks of dust on the lens will do no harm at all. Frequent careless cleaning with a handkerchief can cause considerable damage that is progressive and insidious. If dust or sand does find its way into the camera in significant quantities, you would be better advised to take it to a competent mechanic for complete overhaul. The same applies if you are so unfortunate as to drop your camera into water, particularly salt water. The chances are, in both cases, that at least partial dismantling will be necessary to get the water, sand, etc. out of inaccessible parts and to effect thorough cleaning and regreasing.

When carrying the camera, keep it close to the body on a tight strap so that it does not swing out into brick walls or tree trunks. Whether you use the so-called ever-ready case or not is a matter of personal preference. It is useful for storage and transport but rather cumbersome when actually shooting. Few now open and close easily and even when you can remove the front portion you have a problem in disposing of it.

There are similar difficulties with lens cases and there is a lot to be said for carrying your equipment in polythene bags in a small gadget bag, leaving the cases at home for storage purposes. All these cases and the gadget bag itself tend to attract dust and fluff and the polythene bag offers better protection.

Never, under any circumstances, attempt to repair a camera that is malfunctioning unless you are absolutely certain that you know what you are doing. Camera repairs are expensive but they can become a great deal more expensive if inexpert repairs are attempted first.

Glossary

Aberration. Failing in the ability of a lens to produce a true image. There are many forms of aberration and the lens designer can often correct some only by allowing others to remain. Generally, the more expensive the lens, the less its aberrations.

Angle of view. The extent of the view taken in by a lens. For any particular film size, it varies with the focal length of the lens. Usually expressed on the diagonal of the image area.

Aperture. The opening in the lens, usually provided by an adjustable iris diaphragm, though which light passes. See Limiting aperture, Effective aperture, *f*-number.

Aperture priority. Automatic exposure system in which the lens aperture is set by the photographer, and the camera sets the shutter speed. Can be used in the stop-down mode with any lens that does not interfere with the metering system.

Artificial light. Light from a man-made source, usually restricted to studio, photolamp and domestic lighting. When used to describe film (also known as Type A or Type B) invariably means these types of lighting.

ASA. Film speed rating defined by the American National Standards Institute.

Automatic iris. Lens diaphragm which is controlled by a mechanism in the camera body coupled to the shutter release. The diaphragm closes to any preset value before the shutter opens and returns to the fully open position when the shutter closes.

Balanced. Description applied to colour films to indicate their ability to produce acceptable colour response in various types of lighting. The films normally available are balanced for daylight (5500–6000K), photolamps (3400K) or studio lamps (3200K).

Cadmium sulphide (CdS). Photo conductive material used in exposure meters as alternative to selenium-based or silicon blue photocells. Its electrical resistance decreases as the light falling on it increases. Cds meters use current from an external power source, such as a battery.

Camera shake. Movement of camera caused by unsteady hold or support, vibration, etc., leading, particularly at slower shutter speeds, to a blurred image on the film. It is a major cause of unsharp pictures, especially with long focus lenses.

Capacitor. Electrical component once more commonly known as a condenser. Stores electrical energy supplied by a power source and can discharge it more rapidly than the source itself. Used in flash equipment, providing reliable bulb firing even from weak batteries, and supplying the surge needed for electronic flash tubes.

Cassette. Light-trapped film container used with 35 mm cameras.

Cast. Abnormal colouring of an image produced by departure from recommended exposure or processing conditions with a transparency film, or when making a colour print. Can also be caused by reflection within the subject as from a hat on to the face.

Click stop. Ball bearing and recess or similar construction used to enable shutter speeds, aperture values, etc. to be set by touch.

Colour negative. Film designed to produce colour image with both tones and colours reversed for subsequent printing to a positive image, usually on paper.

Colour reversal. Film designed to produce a normal colour positive image on the film exposed in the camera for subsequent viewing by transmitted light or projection on to a screen.

Colour temperature. Description of the colour of a light-source by comparing it with the colour of light emitted by a (theoretical) perfect radiator at a particular temperature expressed in kelvins (K). Thus "photographic daylight" has a colour temperature of about 5500K. Photographic tungsten lights have colour temperatures of either 3400K or 3200K depending on their construction.

Component. Part of a compound lens consisting of one element (single lens) or more than one element cemented or otherwise joined together. A lens may therefore be described as 4-element, 3-component when two of the elements are cemented together.

Computer flash. Electronic flash guns which sense the light reflected from the subject, and cut off their output when they have received sufficient light for correct exposure. Most units must be used on or close to the camera for direct lighting only. and the camera lens must be set to a specific aperture (or a small range of apertures) determined by the speed of the film in use.

Condenser. Generally a simple lens used to collect light and concentrate it on a particular area, as in enlarger or projector. Frequently in the form of two plano-convex lenses in a metal housing. A condenser, normally of the fresnel type, is used to ensure even illumination of the viewing screens on SLR cameras.

Contrast. Tonal difference. More often used to compare original and reproduction. A negative may be said to be contrasty if it shows fewer, more widely spaced tones than in the original.

Delayed action. Mechanism delaying the opening of the shutter for some seconds after the release has been operated. Also known as self-timer.

Depth of field. The distance between the nearest and farthest planes in a scene that a lens can reproduce with acceptable sharpness. Varies with effective aperture (and thus with focal length at any particular *f*-number) focused distance and the standards set for acceptable sharpness.

Developer. Solution used to make visible the image produced by allowing light to fall on the light-sensitive material. The basic constituent is a developing agent which reduces the light-struck silver halide to metallic silver. Colour developers include chemicals which produce coloured dyes coincidentally with reduction of the silver halides.

Diaphragm. Device consisting of thin overlapping metal leaves pivoting outwards to form a circular opening of variable size. Used to control light transmission through a lens.

DIN. Film speed rating defined by the Deutscher Normenausschuss (German standards organisation).

Effective aperture. The diameter of the bundle of light rays striking the first lens element that actually pass through the lens at any given diaphragm setting.

Electronic flash. Light source based on electrical discharge across two electrodes in a gas-filled tube. Usually designed to provide light approximating to daylight.

Element. Single lens used in association with others to form a compound construction.

Emulsion. Suspension of light-sensitive silver salts in gelatin.

Exposure. The act of allowing light to reach the light-sensitive emulsion of the photographic material. Also refers to the amount (duration and intensity) of light which reaches the film.

Exposure factor. A figure by which the exposure indicated for an average subject and/or processing should be multiplied to allow for non-average conditions. Usually applied to filters, occasionally to lighting, processing, etc. Not normally used with through-the-lens exposure meters.

Exposure meter. Instrument containing light sensitive substance which indicates aperture and shutter speed settings required.

Extension bellows. Device used to provide the additional separation between lens and film required for close-up photography. Consists of extendible bellows and mounting plates at front and rear to fit the lens and camera body respectively.

Extension tubes. Metal tubes used to obtain the additional separation between lens and film for close-up photography. They are fitted with screw thread or bayonet mounts to suit various lens mounts.

f-number. Numerical expression of the light-transmitting power of a lens. Calculated from the focal length of the lens divided by the diameter of the bundle of light rays entering the lens and passing through the aperture in the iris diaphragm.

Film base. Flexible support on which light sensitive emulsion is coated.

Filter. A piece of material which restricts the transmission of radiation. Generally coloured to absorb light of certain colours. Can be used over light sources or over the camera lens. Camera lens filters are usually glass—either dyed or sandwiching a piece of gelatin—in a screw-in filter holder.

Fisheye lens. Ultra-wide angle lens giving 180° angle of view. Basically produces a circular image—on 35 mm, 5–9 mm lenses showing whole image, 15–17 mm lenses giving a rectangular image fitting just inside the circle, thus representing 180° across the diagonal.

Fixer. Solution, usually based on sodium thiosulphate, in which films or prints are immersed after development to convert the unexposed silver halides in the emulsion to soluble products that can be washed out. This prevents subsequent deterioration of the image.

Flashbulb. Light source based on ignition of combustible metal wire in a gas-filled transparent envelope. Popular sizes are usually blue-coated to give light approximating to daylight.

Flashcube. Self-contained unit comprising four small flashbulbs with own reflectors. Designed to rotate in special camera socket as film is wound on. Can be used in a special adapter on cameras without the socket, but will not rotate automatically.

Focal length. Distance from a lens to the image it produces of a very distant subject. With a compound lens the point from which it is measured depends on the construction of the lens. It is within the lens with those of normal construction, but may be in front of telephoto lenses, or behind inverted telephotos. Whatever the lens construction, the focal length determines the size of the image formed.

Focus. Generally, the act of adjusting a lens to produce a sharp image. In a camera, this is effected by moving the lens bodily towards or away from the film or by moving the front part of the lens towards or away from the rear part, thus altering its focal length.

Format. Shape and size of image provided by camera or presented in final print or transparency. Governed in the camera by the opening at the rear of the body over which the film passes or is placed. The standard 35 mm format is 36×24 mm; half-frame, 18×24 mm; 126 size, 28×28 mm; 110, 17×13 mm; standard rollfilm (120 size), $2\frac{1}{4} \times 2\frac{1}{4}$ in.

Fresnel. Pattern of a special form of condenser lens consisting of a series of concentric stepped rings, each being a section of a convex surface which would, if continued, form a much thicker lens. Used on focusing screens to distribute image brightness evenly over the screen.

Full aperture metering. TTL metering systems in which the camera simulates the effect of stopping down the lens when the aperture ring is turned, while leaving the diaphragm at full aperture to give full focusing screen brilliance. The meter must be "programmed" with the actual full aperture, and the diaphragm ring setting.

Grain. Minute metallic silver deposit, forming in quantity the photographic image. The individual grain is never visible, even in an enlargement, but the random nature of their distribution in the emulsion causes over-lapping, or clumping, which can lead to graininess in the final image.

Graininess. Visible evidence of the granular structure of a photographic reproduction. Influenced by exposure, development, contrast characteristics and surface of printing paper, emulsion structure and degree of enlargement. Basically increases with increasing film speed.

Grey card. Tone used as representative of mid-tone of average subject. The standard grey card reflects 18 per cent of the light falling on it.

Guide number. Figure allocated to a light source, usually flash, representing the product of aperture number and light-to-subject distance required for correct exposure.

Halation. The production of "halos" round bright spots in an image, by light reflecting from the back of the film-base. General film bases are given a light-absorbing coat—the anti-halation back—to prevent this.

Highlight. Small, very bright part of image or object. Highlights should generally be pure white, although the term is sometimes used to describe the lightest tones of a picture, which, in that case, may need to contain some detail.

Image. Two-dimensional reproduction of a subject formed by a lens. When formed on a surface, i.e. a ground-glass screen, it is a real image; if in space, i.e. when the screen is removed, it is an aerial image. The image seen through a telescope, optical viewfinder, etc. cannot be focused on a surface without the aid of another optical system and is a virtual image.

Incident light. Light falling on a surface as opposed to the light reflected by it.

Infinity. Infinite distance. In practice, a distance so great that any object at that distance will be reproduced sharply if the lens is set at its infinity position, i.e. one focal length from the film.

Interchangeable lens. Lens designed to be readily attached to and detached from a camera.

Inverted telephoto lens. Lens constructed so that the back focus (distance from rear of lens to film) is greater than the focal length of the lens. This construction allows room for mirror movement when short focus lenses are fitted to SLR cameras.

Iris. Strictly, iris diaphragm. Device consisting of thin overlapping metal leaves pivoting outwards to form a circular opening of variable size to control light transmission through a lens.

Leader. Part of film attached to camera take-up spool. 35 mm film usually has a leader of the shape originally designed for bottom-loading Leica cameras, although most cameras simply need a short taper.

Lighting ratio. The ratio of the brightness of light falling on the subject from the main (key) light and other (fill) lights. A ratio of about 3:1 is normal for colour photography, greater ratios may be used for effect in black-and-white work.

Limiting aperture. The actual size of the aperture formed by the iris diaphragm at any setting. Determines, but usually differs from, the effective aperture.

Long-focus. Lens of relatively long focal length designed to provide a narrower angle of view than the normal or standard lens, which generally has an angle of view, expressed on the diagonal of the film format, of about 45 deg. The long focus lens thus takes in less of the view in front of it but on an enlarged scale.

Magicube. Special form of flashcube which is fired by mechanical (not electrical) means. Can be used only on cameras fitted with the appropriate socket.

Manual iris. Diaphragm controlled directly by a calibrated ring on the lens barrel.

Microprism. Minute glass or plastic structure of multiple prisms set in a view-finder screen to act as a focusing aid. Breaks up an out-of-focus subject into a shimmer but images a focused subject clearly. Will not work satisfactorily at lens apertures smaller than f 5·6.

Mirror lens. Lens in which some (usually two) of the elements are curved mirrors. This construction produces comparatively lightweight short fat long focus lenses. They cannot be fitted with a normal diaphragm.

Modelling. Representation by lighting of the three-dimensional nature of an original in a two-dimensional reproduction.

Neutral density filter. Grey filter that absorbs light of all colours equally and thus has no effect on colour rendering with colour film or tonal values with black and white film. Primarily used with mirror lenses or to enable large apertures to be used in bright light conditions.

Parallax. Apparent change in position of an object due to changed viewpoint. In a camera with separate viewfinder, the taking lens and the viewfinder view an object from slightly different positions. At close range, the image produced on the film is significantly different from that seen in the viewfinder. Completely eliminated in single-lens reflex cameras.

Perspective. Size, position and distance relationship between objects. Varies according to viewpoint so that objects at different distances from the observer appear to be closer together with increasing distance. Thus, a long-focus lens used at long range and a wide-angle lens used very close up provide images very different from that of the standard lens used at a normal working distance.

Photolamp (3400K). Photographic lamp giving more light than a normal lamp of the same wattage, at the expense of filament life. Often referred to by the trade mark Photoflood. Are used with type A colour films.

Plane. Level surface. Used in photography chiefly in respect to focal plane, an imaginary level surface perpendicular to the lens axis in which the lens is intended to form an image. When the camera is loaded the focal plane is occupied by the film surface.

Polarized light. Light waves vibrating in one plane only as opposed to the multi-directional vibrations of normal rays. Natural effect produced by some reflecting surfaces, such as glass, water, polished wood, etc., but can also be simulated by placing a special screen in front of the light source. The transmission of polarized light is restricted by using a screen at an angle to the plane of polarization.

Preset iris. Diaphragm with two setting rings or one ring that can be moved to two positions. One is click-stopped, but does not affect the iris, the other moves freely and alters the aperture. The required aperture is preset on the first ring, and the iris closed down with the second just before exposure.

Rangefinder. Instrument for measuring distances from a given point, usually based on slightly separated views of the scene provided by mirrors or prisms. May be built into non-reflex cameras. Single-lens reflexes may have prismatic range-finders built into their focusing screens.

Refill. Length of film usually for loading into 35 mm cassettes in total darkness. Daylight refills are not now generally available.

Relative aperture. Numerical expression of effective aperture, also known as ƒ-number. Obtained by dividing focal length by diameter of effective aperture.

Resolution. Ability of film, lens or both in conjunction to reproduce fine detail. Commonly measured in lines per millimetre as ascertained by photographing, or focusing the lens on, a specially constructed test target. The resolution of modern lenses and films is so high that differences have no bearing on normal photography except with the simplest lenses and fastest films.

Safelight. Light source consisting of housing, lamp and screen of a colour that will not affect the photographic material in use. Safelight screens are available in various colours and sizes for specific applications.

Scale. Focusing method consisting of set of marks to indicate distances at which a lens is focused. May be engraved around the lens barrel, on the focusing control or on the camera body.

Screen. In a camera, the surface upon which the lens projects an image for viewfinding and, usually, focusing purposes. In SLR cameras, almost universally a fresnel screen with a fine-ground surface. Often incorporates a microprism or split-image rangefinder.

Selenium. Light-sensitive substance which, when used in a barrier-layer construction, generates electrical current when exposed to light. Used in exposure meters. Needs no external power supply.

Self-timer. Mechanism delaying the opening of the shutter for some seconds after the release has been operated. Also known as delayed action.

Semi-automatic iris. Diaphragm mechanism which closes down to the taking aperture when the shutter is released, but must be manually re-opened to full aperture.

Sensitivity. Expression of the nature of a photographic emulsion's response to light. Can be concerned with degree of sensitivity as expressed by film speed or response to light of various colours (spectral sensitivity).

Sharpness. Clarity of the photographic image in terms of focus and contrast. Largely subjective but can be measured to some extent by assessing adjacency effects, i.e. the abruptness of the change in density between adjoining areas of different tone value.

Short-focus. Lens of relatively short focal length designed to provide a wider angle of view than the normal or standard lens, which generally has an angle of view, expressed on the diagonal of the film format, of about 45 deg. The short focus lens takes in more of the view in front of it but on a smaller scale.

Shutter priority. Automatic exposure systems in which the shutter speed is set by the photographer, and the camera selects the lens aperture appropriate to the film speed and the light reflected from the subject. Such systems must meter the light at full aperture and use specially connected lenses.

Silicon. Light-sensitive substance which generates a minute current when exposed to light. Requires no external power source, but, in exposure meters, uses an externally powered amplifier.

Split-image. Form of rangefinder image, bisected so that the two halves of the image are aligned only when the correct object distance is set on the instrument or, in the case of a coupled rangefinder, when the lens is correctly focused. SLR cameras may have a prismatic split-image system in their viewing screen. Works on the same principle as a microprism, and is restricted to apertures of f 5·6 or greater.

Stabilizer. Alternative to fixer where permanence is not required. Used in automatic processing machines and can now provide prints that will not deteriorate noticeably over many months if kept away from strong light.

Stop-down metering. TTL metering in which the light is measured at the picture-taking aperture. As the meter just measures the light passing through the lens, there is no need for any lens-camera interconnections.

Studio lamps (3200K). Tungsten or tungsten halogen lamps designed for studio use. Have a longer life than photolamps, but a lower specific output and colour temperature. Are used with type B films.

Supplementary lens. Generally a simple positive (converging) lens used in front of the camera lens to enable it to focus at close range. The effect is to provide a lens of shorter focal length without altering the lens-film separation, thus giving the extra extension required for close focusing.

Synchronisation. Concerted action of shutter opening and closing of electrical contacts to fire a flashbulb or electronic flash at the correct moment to make most efficient use of the light output. Roughly speaking, FP or M-synchronisation is constructed to fire flashbulbs just before the shutter is fully open, allowing a build-up time, and X-synchronisation fires electronic flash exactly at the moment the shutter is fully open.

Telephoto. Special form of long-focus lens construction in which the back focus (distance from rear of lens to film) is much less than the focal length of the lens.

Through-the-lens (TTL). Type of exposure meter built into the camera body and reading through the camera lens. May measure either at full aperture or at picture taking aperture.

Type A. Colour film balanced for use with photolamps (3400K).

Type B. Colour film balanced for use with studio lamps (3200K).

Ultra-wide angle lens. Extra-wide angle lens, usually those with an angle of view greater than 90°. For 35 mm cameras the description usually applies to lenses of shorter focal length than about 24 mm.

Variable focus lens. Lens of which the focal length can be continuously varied between set limits. The lens must be refocused with each change in focal length.

Viewfinder. Device or system indicating the field of view encompassed by the camera lens. The term is sometimes used as a description of the type of camera that does not use reflex or "straight-through" viewing systems and therefore has to have a separate viewfinder.

Vignetting. Underexposure of image corners produced deliberately by shading or unintentionally by inappropriate equipment, such as unsuitable lens hood or badly designed lens. A common fault of wide-angle lenses, owing to reflection, cut-off, etc. of some of the very oblique rays. May be caused in some long-focus lenses by the length of the lens barrel.

Wide-angle. Lens designed to provide a wider angle of view than the normal or standard lens. Generally has an angle of view, expressed on the diagonal of the film format, of about 60 deg. or more. The wide-angle lens thus takes in more of the view in front of it but on a reduced scale.

Zoom lens. Lens of which the focal length can be continuously varied within stated limits while maintaining the focus originally set.